REPENTANCE

EXPLAINED AND ENFORCED

A SERIOUS APPEAL TO EVERY MAN'S CONSCIENCE ON ITS NATURE, NECESSITY, AND EVIDENCES

I tell you, Nay: but, except ye repent, ye shall all likewise perish. – Luke 13:5

BY J. THORNTON

1834

© The Old Paths Publications
2021

REPENTANCE

EXPLAINED AND ENFORCED

BEING

A SERIOUS APPEAL TO EVERY MAN'S CONSCIENCE
ON ITS NATURE, NECESSITY, AND EVIDENCES

BY J. THORNTON

WITH A NEW INTRODUCTION AND APPENDIX

I tell you, Nay: but, except ye repent, ye shall all likewise perish. – Luke 13:5

NEW HAVEN:

PUBLISHED BY L. H. YOUNG, 1834
No. 1, Exchange Place.

Republished by The Old Paths Publications
February 2021

ISBN: 978-1-7365344-5-8

ADDRESS ALL INQUIRES TO:
The Old Paths Publications
142 Gold Flume Way
Cleveland, GA 30528
www.theoldpathspublications.com
TOP@theoldpathspublications.com

ACKNOWLEDGEMENTS

A special thank you is due to Pastor Jon Harwood and Solid Rock Baptist Church of Calgary, Canada, for financially providing for the publication of this book. Mr. Frank Crawford checked the entire book text and re-typed the original edition, making corrections for minor printing errors, and added an expanded Table of Contents to prepare it for publication. Dr. H. D. Williams of The Old Paths Publications Inc. kindly offered to publish this classic work.

The Old Paths Publications appreciates the liberty granted to reformat this great work.

H. D. Williams, M.D., Ph.D.
President, The Old Paths Publications, Inc.
Copies may be ordered on our website as well as complimentary books and tracts:
http://www.theoldpathspublications.com/Pages/BookStore.htm

INTRODUCTION
TO THE NEW HAVEN EDITION

The frequent calls for the following work, and the testimony borne to its merits, by many faithful and experienced clergymen, who have made use of it in their parishes, have induced the publisher to offer a new edition, in the present cheap and convenient form.

The principal portion of the Author's Preface, being wholly inapplicable to the state of things in this country, it has been deemed advisable to retain only so much of it as may be necessary to explain the object of the work. With this omission, and the addition of a few short forms of prayer, which may be found convenient and useful in directing the devotions of the honest and anxious inquirer, this edition presents the work precisely in its original form. The six chapters which constitute the entire body of the work, remain without the slightest alteration.

It was the design of the author of this work, to furnish a plain and concise treatise on one of the most important subjects connected with the doctrines of the gospel: – "to open the nature – to prove the necessity – and to point out the means and evidences of evangelical repentance." "Many (the author admits) have written well on the doctrine of repentance; but the subject is mingled with others, in voluminous works." He felt the necessity, therefore, of preparing a treatise on this all-important topic, in a small compass, and in a plain style – that it might thus obtain a general circulation among all classes of people. The giving away or lending of books of this description, is among the means of promoting the cause of religion at the present day; and the author correctly remarks, that "those who diligently and prudently use these means, will seldom fail to see some happy effects produced; and much of the seed which is thus sown, may

INTRODUCTION

spring up when the hands that scattered it are mouldering in the dust."

"If this small work (adds the author) should be blessed of God as a means of exciting a deep and serious concern about the ONE THING NEEDFUL, in any who receive it, I shall think myself well rewarded. May that Being, from whom cometh every blessing, cause the influence of his grace to accompany it to many hearts."

TABLE OF CONTENTS

ACKNOWLEDGEMENTS 3
INTRODUCTION TO THE NEW HAVEN EDITION 4
CHAPTER I: ON THE STATE OF THE IMPENITENT 10
   TO SHOW THE STATE OF THE IMPENITENT 12
      THE IMPENITENT ARE IN A STATE OF SPIRITUAL DARKNESS 12
      THE IMPENITENT ARE IN A STATE OF DISTANCE FROM GOD 14
      THE IMPENITENT ARE IN A STATE OF DEEP POLLUTION 16
      THE IMPENITENT ARE IN A STATE OF GUILT AND CONDEMNATION 18
      THE IMPENITENT ARE IN A STATE OF BONDAGE AND MISERY 19
      THE PROMOTION OF SELF-EXAMINATION AND HUMILITY 21
CHAPTER 2: ON THE NATURE OF REPENTANCE 26
   THE NATURE OF TRUE REPENTANCE 27
   A SINCERE PENITENT HAS A CHANGE OF MIND 27
   A Sincere Penitent has Right Views of God 27
   A Sincere Penitent has Right Views and New Thoughts of Christ ... 29
   A Sincere Penitent has New Thoughts of His Own Soul 29
   REPENTANCE IS CONTRITION OF HEART 30
   True Repentance is a State of Mind 31
   REPENTANCE IS DEEP SELF-ABHORRENCE 35
      A View of the Number of His Sins 35
      A View of the Greatness of His Sins 36
      A View of the Fruits and Effects of His Sins 38
   NEEDFUL CAUTIONS CONCERNING TRUE REPENTANCE 39
      Do not Put Confession of Sin in the Place of Repentance 39
      Do not Mistake the Occasional Meltings of Natural Affection, for Repentance 40
      When You Begin to Feel Some Serious Concern, be not Eager to Get Rid of Your Uneasiness by Improper Means 41
      Do not rest content with what the world calls morality 42
CHAPTER 3: ON THE NECESSITY OF REPENTANCE 44
   REPENTANCE IS ABSOLUTELY, UNIVERSALLY AND IMMEDIATELY NECESSARY 44
      REPENTANCE IS ABSOLUTELY NECESSARY 45

TABLE OF CONTENTS

    Without Repentance, It is Impossible to Obtain Heaven............45
    Without Repentance, It is Impossible to Avoid Hell 46
REPENTANCE IS *UNIVERSALLY* NECESSARY............. 49
    To the Profligate and Presumptuous 49
    To the Negligent and Careless 52
    To the Self-Righteous and Hypocritical..54
REPENTANCE IS *IMMEDIATELY* NECESSARY............ 56
    Presuming that You shall Yet live Many Years..............................57
    Presuming on the Mercy of God 59
    A Presumption, Built upon Remarkable Instances of *Late* Conversion 60
AN ANSWER TO TWO OBJECTIONS 61
CHAPTER 4: ON THE MEANS OF PROMOTING REPENTANCE 64
THE READING OF THE HOLY SCRIPTURES, AND OTHER GOOD BOOKS.. 66
THE PREACHING OF THE GOSPEL.......................... 69
THE USE OF PRUDENT COUNSELS, AND FAITHFUL, AFFECTIONATE REPROOFS.................................... 71
AFFLICTION 72
ANSWERING NOTIONS AGAINST THE MEANS USED FOR PRODUCING REPENTANCE 74
    The Notion I oppose, is Contrary to Scripture 74
    The Notion I oppose, is Contrary to Experience 75
    The Notion I here oppose is Contrary to Common Sense...............75
    The Notion which opposes the Use of Means to Promote Repentance, is Agreeable to the Will of the Devil 76
REPENTANCE IS A DUTY, AS WELL AS A PRIVILEGE.. 77
IN ORDER TO PROMOTE REPENTANCE 80
    Meditate on the Shortness of Time, and the Awful Importance of Eternity...80
    Meditate on the Glorious Perfections of God.................................81
    Meditate on the Life, the Amazing Love, and the Sin-Atoning Death of Jesus Christ 83
    Meditate Seriously and Daily on the Wonderful Love of Christ. 84
CHAPTER 5: ON THE EVIDENCES OF REPENTANCE 86

WHAT ARE NO EVIDENCES OR PROOFS OF TRUE REPENTANCE ... 86
A Great Deal of Labor to Keep up Fair Appearances ... 87
Sudden Terrors, or Melancholy Thoughts ... 88
Lively Joys, and Confident Hopes ... 89
WHAT ARE THE EVIDENCES OF REAL REPENTANCE .. 90
A True Penitent will Forsake His Sin ... 90
A True Penitent Renounces the World ... 94
A True Penitent Resists the Devil ... 96
A True Penitent Loves Christ, and Longs to be Conformed to His Likeness ... 99
I SHALL MAKE A FEW OBSERVATIONS ... 102
Highly Important that You should know Whether You are Truly Penitent or Not ... 102
Very Necessary to be Careful in Examining Yourself ... 103
PERSONALLY APPLYING THE EVIDENCES OF REPENTANCE ... 104
(If) You are Fully Convinced that You are Yet in a State of Impenitence? ... 105
If You have Some Evidences of Repentance ... 106

CHAPTER 6: ON THE ENCOURAGEMENTS GIVEN TO THE PENITENT ... 108
THE SCRIPTURES PROMISE *PARDON* TO THE PENITENT ... 109
God Commands You to accept Pardon ... 110
God Invites You to accept of Pardon ... 111
(God) Pleads with You to accept Pardon ... 112
God Points You to the Blood of Atonement, by which it was procured ... 113
God Points You to the Intercession of His Son ... 114
God Points You to Those Who have obtained the Precious Blessing ... 115
THE SCRIPTURES OFFER TO THE PENITENT, ADOPTION INTO THE HOUSEHOLD OF GOD ... 118
THE SCRIPTURES PROMISE TO THE PENITENT THE INFLUENCE OF THE HOLY SPIRIT ... 123
It is the Office of the Holy Spirit to Enlighten the Soul ... 125

TABLE OF CONTENTS

    It is the Office of the Holy Spirit to Sanctify the Soul 126
    It is the Office of the Holy Spirit to Comfort the Soul 127
SET THESE ENCOURAGEMENTS BEFORE YOU 129
    To Quicken You in Your Duties, and Animate You Amidst all Your Fears and Foes 129
    To Support You Amidst all Your Foes and Fears 130
    Set Your Hand to the Covenant of God, and Solemnly Surrender your Soul to Him 131
PRAYERS 134
    PRAYER FOR EXAMINATION 134
    FOR TRUE CONTRITION 134
    FOR PARDON 135
    FOR GRACE 136
    FOR PREPARATION FOR ETERNITY 137
APPENDIX 138
    BACKGROUND 138
    RELATED STUDY ITEMS ON THE OLD PATHS PUBLICATIONS WEBSITE 138

CHAPTER I
ON THE STATE OF THE IMPENITENT

I will tell you, reader, in the beginning, what is my design in this little book: I do not intend to amuse you with curious questions, or engage you in fierce disputes, and vain janglings; but to show you the things that belong to your peace. You must soon die, and bid farewell to the world. You are gliding down the stream of time, into a shoreless and bottomless ocean. It is clear, from the Word of God, that after death you must be either eternally happy, or eternally miserable. It is as plain as words can make it, that if you go on hardened in sin to the last, your precious immortal soul will be certainly lost, and lost forever. I therefore beg your serious attention to the subject of repentance. No subject is more frequently and urgently pressed upon men in the Holy Scriptures. Every messenger that God has sent to perishing sinners, has brought a call to repentance. Every instance of the careless and profane cut off by death, is a loud call to the living. Every affliction in your own person, is a call from God to repentance.

Think of the value and duration of the soul. Luther declares this life to be but a little piece of life everlasting. When you have passed over your narrow span of time, you must immediately enter upon a boundless eternity. As you sow in this world, you must reap in that which is to come. While, therefore, I set before you the nature and necessity of repentance, I shall use great plainness of speech. I would keep back nothing that may be profitable to you, but faithfully declare the whole counsel of God. If I make use of strong and pointed language, it is because I most ardently wish to arouse you to a true sense of your danger, and lead you in the way of salvation. Look into the scriptures of the Old Testament, and see with what earnestness and solemnity the prophets exhorted the

CHAPTER 1: ON THE STATE OF THE IMPENITENT

thoughtless, the worldly minded, and the wicked, to forsake their sins, and cast themselves upon the mercy of a pardoning God. Look into the New Testament, and see with what plainness, with what melting compassion, with what burning zeal, Christ and his apostles warned the guilty to flee from the wrath to come, and lay hold on eternal life.

We read in Luke 13:1-5,

There were present at that season some that told him of the Galilaeans, whose blood Pilate had mingled with their sacrifices. And Jesus answering said unto them, Suppose ye that these Galilaeans were sinners above all the Galilaeans, because they suffered such things? I tell you, Nay: but, except ye repent, ye shall all likewise perish. Or those eighteen, upon whom the tower in Siloam fell, and slew them, think ye that they were sinners above all men that dwelt in Jerusalem? I tell you, Nay: but, except ye repent, ye shall all likewise perish.

Here we see how ready men are to put away the weighty concerns of religion from themselves, and think or speak only of other persons. They are willing that blame should be laid anywhere, rather than at their own doors. They shun the light, and labor to shake off those convictions which begin to trouble the conscience. In this scripture, our Lord directs his piercing words to every heart. He also teaches us the use we ought to make of any remarkable events of providence which takes place in the world, and especially in our own neighborhood. In no part of the Bible is the absolute necessity of repentance more forcibly insisted on, than in this passage. As, however, a man must see his danger before he will inquire for a refuge, and his disease, before he will seek for a remedy, I shall proceed.

TO SHOW THE STATE OF THE IMPENITENT

To fix a deeper impression on the mind, the scriptures represent the unconverted by various comparisons. Thus we find the impenitent described as in a state of spiritual darkness, of distance from God, of deep pollution, of guilt and condemnation, of bondage and misery.

THE IMPENITENT ARE IN A STATE OF SPIRITUAL DARKNESS

It is said:

This is life eternal, to know the only true God, and Jesus Christ whom he hath sent. But sin is a dark cloud upon the mind, a thick veil drawn over the heart, which excludes the precious light of divine truth. But the natural man receiveth not the things of the Spirit of God: for they are foolishness unto him; neither can he know them, because they are spiritually discerned. (1Corinthians 2:14).

To one who is in this state, the clearest displays of the power, wisdom, justice, and goodness of God; and the fullest manifestations of the love, compassion, faithfulness, and glory of Christ, are only as the beauties of a fine prospect to a blind man. While the understanding, which is the window of the mind, remains shut, all within must be dreary darkness. When there is no motion of love and gratitude in the heart, no breathing of fervent prayer from the lips towards God, the soul is dead in trespasses and sins. How strong, and yet how just, is the language of the prophet: *Darkness hath covered the earth, and gross darkness the people.* What can more truly describe the ignorance and stupidity of the carnal mind, than these words?

And is this, reader, your unhappy state? Be not offended at this serious question, but examine whether it be so or not. It is possible you may be proud of your

CHAPTER 1: ON THE STATE OF THE IMPENITENT

knowledge, and yet, in spiritual matters, continue as blind as the mole that grovels in the earth. The footsteps of God are printed on the works of creation, and yet you do not see those footsteps, and admire. The hand of God is stretched out, guiding all the affairs of providence, giving you daily bread and hourly protection, and yet you do not see that hand, and thankfully adore. The face of God, the reconciled countenance of the Father, shines as in a glass, in the gospel, and yet you do not see it, and heartily rejoice. The unsearchable riches of Christ, and the everlasting glories of heaven, are opened by the promises, and still you neither see their value, nor seek them. Are not these proofs that the understanding is darkened? Seneca, in a letter to a friend, says, "My wife keeps a poor silly girl, who all of a sudden lost her sight; and (which may seem incredible, but is very true) she does not know that she is blind; but is every now and then asking her governess to lead her abroad, saying the house is dark. Now what we laugh at in this poor creature, we may observe happens to us all. No man knows that he is covetous or insatiable. Yet with this difference, the blind seek somebody to lead them, but we are content to wander without a guide."

If you beheld a man walking unconcerned near the edge of a deep whirlpool, would you not think him blind or mad? Would you not fly to snatch him back from destruction? And what can be a more full proof of spiritual blindness, than a total indifference to the dangers that threaten the soul? If fire comes so near your house or goods, that you have reason to fear they will be consumed, you use every means to secure them. But though the fire of God's wrath is kindling to destroy the soul, you neither dread nor see the danger. If the mind were not grossly darkened, how could you thoughtlessly dance and sport on the borders of the bottomless pit? It is true, light is come into the world, you live amidst the full blaze of gospel day, and yet you love darkness rather than light.

> O, If thou hadst known, even thou, at least in this thy day, the things which belong unto thy peace! but now they are hid from thine eyes. (Luke 19:42).

THE IMPENITENT ARE IN A STATE OF DISTANCE FROM GOD

In the scriptures all are represented as wanderers from God.

> All we like sheep have gone astray; we have turned every one to his own way. (Isaiah 53:6). We have forsaken the fountain of living waters, and hewed out cisterns, broken cisterns, that can hold no water (Jeremiah 2:13).

Since Adam fell, every son and daughter of Adam is averse to good and inclined to evil. Not only is the understanding darkened, but the will is perverted, and the affections are corrupted. Instead of seeking happiness from God, the everlasting spring of all blessings, we naturally seek it in the foolish devices and imaginations of our own hearts.

This distance from God, our Lord sets forth in a just comparison, Matthew 7:13 and 14.

> Wide is the gate, and broad is the way, that leadeth to destruction, and many there be that go in thereat.

Let me beg you to pay a particular attention to this remarkable scripture. In the broad way, there are many separate paths, which all run to the same dreadful end. The inclinations and passions of ungodly men may lead them to different follies and vices, while they are all living without Christ and far from righteousness. In the broad way is the path of *gaiety*, full of amusements and diversions. What glittering toys! what alluring vanities! what tempting baits! are here held out to catch the careless, or to entice and delude the young. This flowery path, furnished so plentifully with enchanting

CHAPTER 1: ON THE STATE OF THE IMPENITENT

charms, is traveled by all who are *lovers of pleasures more than lovers of God.* Near the path of *gaiety*, is the path of *profligacy*, in which are prodigals, wasting their substance in riotous living; adulterers and drunkards, glorying in their shame; liars and swearers, whose mouths are full of falsehood, cursing, and bitterness; gamesters and thieves, who live by plunder and violence, neither fearing God, nor regarding man. In the broad way, is the path of *self-righteousness*. This indeed is very lofty, and has a fair and showy appearance, but it is exceedingly dangerous. Here are the proud and high-minded, who boast of their good works, and dream of obtaining heaven by their own fancied merit. In the broad way are the crooked paths of *deceit*, full of traps and snares, and covered pit-falls. Here travel smooth-tongued dissemblers, and painted hypocrites. The path of covetousness is crowded with sordid worldlings, heaping up riches and lading themselves with thick clay. Now, all these paths lead to destruction. This is not any airy fancy, but a certain fact. The words of Christ will be found true, whether you believe them or not. Consider, reader, whether you are not yet in this broad way. It is a thing which may be known, and ought to be determined without any delay. Perhaps you have passed from one path to another, but are still rushing on in the downward and dangerous road. O, stop, presumptuous sinner, in your mad career! With deepest concern, and the tenderest affection, I would admonish and persuade you. If it were possible for me to save you by force, as the angel laid hold of Lot to lead him out of Sodom, I would gladly do it. But all I can do is, to reason with you, and try every argument and motive the most likely to reach the understanding, and touch the heart. It is probable you have heard many a loud call, and felt many a sharp check, and yet you drive on with fury! Whither are you moving with such hasty strides? What will be the end of your present course? Ah! you are fast going, perhaps far gone toward eternal perdition! There is but a step between you and death; and not a step between death and despair! The voice of heaven calls you to turn to God, from whom you have so deeply revolted. Except you be converted, *and become as a little child, you can in no wise enter into the kingdom of God.*

THE IMPENITENT ARE IN A STATE OF DEEP POLLUTION

There is a generation that are pure in their own eyes, and yet are not washed from their filthiness. It has been said, "Man is a polished mirror, with one slight speck, vanity; and that speck is wiped off by death." According to this fine flattering comparison, sin, it seems, must not be called a blot, nor even a stain, but a speck, a slight speck. According to this fine flattering comparison, sin, it seems, must not be called a blot, nor even a stain, but a speck, a *slight* speck. Let us now examine what the word of God says respecting human nature, in its present state. He who sees into the heart, and will be the judge of all in the last day, must be allowed capable of giving the most just account of man. Turn to Genesis 6:5-12.

> *And God saw that the wickedness of man was great in the earth, and that every imagination of the thoughts of his heart was only evil continually.*

If it should be thought this passage is a proof of the depravity of those only, who lived before the flood, turn to Job 15:14-16.

> *What is man, that he should be clean? and he that is born of a woman, that he should be righteous? Behold, he putteth no trust in his saints; yea, the heavens are not clean in his sight. How much more abominable and filthy is man, which drinketh iniquity like water?*

CHAPTER 1: ON THE STATE OF THE IMPENITENT

Our Lord, who perfectly knew what was in man, opens that fountain of corruption, that forge of iniquity – the carnal heart. Mark 7:21-23.

> *For from within, out of the heart of men, proceed evil thoughts, adulteries, fornications, murders, Thefts, covetousness, wickedness, deceit, lasciviousness, an evil eye, blasphemy, pride, foolishness: All these evil things come from within, and defile the man.*

Nor can it be truly said, that some are free from depravity and sin. Every branch from the stock of Adam is corrupt, though every branch does not bring forth the same quantity of bad fruit. For proof of this, look into Romans 3:9-12.

> *What then? are we better than they? No, in no wise: for we have before proved both Jews and Gentiles, that they are all under sin; As it is written, There is none righteous, no, not one: There is none that understandeth, there is none that seeketh after God. They are all gone out of the way, they are together become unprofitable; there is none that doeth good, no, not one.*

Examine with care the scriptures just repeated. Here is a painting of man, drawn by hands which could not err! It is not suited to flatter self-love and vanity. Sin does not appear as a slight speck; it is the dark coloring that overspreads the whole piece. Do not turn away with levity or scorn, as if it in no way concerned you. I have purposely held up this picture to your view, that you may try if you cannot perceive your own likeness. Yes! you need only look attentively, and you will find every line and every feature, every blot and every blemish in yourself. We may say of the scriptures, which I have been setting before you,

No glass can represent the face More clearly, than these words your case.

REPENTANCE EXPLAINED AND ENFORCED

Chilo, one of the Greek wise men, when he was at the point of death, called his friends to him, and said he could find nothing to repent of, in all his past life; not one fault, except in a single instance, leaning a little too favorably to a friend in judgment. How blind must that man be who cannot see scarlet! Instead of saying you see nothing amiss in your past life, while you examine the scriptures, have you not reason to express yourself in the words of Job to the LORD, "Behold, I am vile; what shall I answer thee?" Are you not fully convinced, that, unless you are washed in the fountain opened for sin and uncleanness, and created anew in the image of Christ, you cannot enter into the kingdom of heaven?

THE IMPENITENT ARE IN A STATE OF GUILT AND CONDEMNATION

It is awful to see a man, who has broken the laws of his country, trembling in his chains, as he hears the sentence which declares him guilty. Condemned to die for his crimes, he feels a thousand horrors, before the hour of execution comes. But that man is in a far more dreadful condition, whom the sentence of the divine law dooms to eternal misery. God, as a God of justice, will not suffer His authority to be trampled upon by the wicked, without calling them to an account for it. Sin, says the apostle John, is the transgression of the law. And God keeps a book of remembrance, in which every vicious deed, every idle word, and every sinful thought, is registered. Now consider that it is said, "Cursed is every one that continueth not in all things written in the book of the law, to do them." And can you believe this without trembling? Is there nothing to alarm you in the wrath of the Almighty? Can you sleep undisturbed, in carnal ease, while the curse of the most high God hangs over your guilty head? But, perhaps, you think yourself clear of the charge brought against you. When the words of the law are repeated, you are ready to cry, "All these things have I kept from my youth up: I never

CHAPTER 1: ON THE STATE OF THE IMPENITENT

committed theft, adultery, nor murder." But is it not possible, you may be too hasty in this matter? Take the trouble of weighing what Christ says of the law in Matthew 5:22-35. There you will find, that slightly uttering the name of God, is profaneness; a wanton look, is adultery; anger, without a just cause, is murder; a grasping eagerness after the world, is covetousness and idolatry. By proceeding in this way, you will be convinced, that, although men's notions of duty and sin are very narrow, *God's commandments are exceeding broad.* If the scriptures are to be believed, it is an undeniable truth, that, by the deeds of the law shall no man living be justified. Not the least room is left for self-righteous pretenses and pleas. Every mouth is stopped, and the whole world is become guilty before God. There is no way of escaping the awful judgments of God, but by faith in the Lord Jesus Christ. Romans 8:1. If you remain still in impenitence and unbelief, you are yet under the curse.

> *He that believeth not, is condemned already, and the wrath of God abideth on him. (John 3:18-36).*

THE IMPENITENT ARE IN A STATE OF BONDAGE AND MISERY

How wretched was the condition of the Israelites in Egypt, when they were not only under the iron rod of Pharaoh, the great tyrant, but also under the smarting scourges of those petty tyrants, the task masters! Well might they sigh and sicken over their hard labors and unpitied woes; but the state of unconverted men is far worse. They sell themselves to do the vilest drudgery. They are the slaves of Satan, and the servants of sin.

Paul declares that those who oppose themselves to the gospel are led captive by the devil at his will. And whither are you likely to be conducted by such a leader? What reward can you expect to receive from such a master? He will draw you on, by little and little, into his snares and fetters, till you are as fast bound as if girt with chains of brass. He will promise many sweets, and give you the apples of Sodom; he will show you the glories of the world, and plunge you in the horrors of despair.

The apostle Peter speaks of some who boast of their liberty, and yet are the servants of corruption. Such persons yield up their powers and members, as instruments of unrighteousness, to sin. Romans 6:13. And, O, what a wretched state is this! Yet every impenitent man is tied down by the base customs of an evil world, and given up to serve divers lusts and pleasures, those cruel task-masters which are never satisfied.

Let it never be forgotten, that sorrow follows sin, as the shadow does the substance. Peter joins together *the bond of iniquity and the gall of bitterness.* Solomon says, *The way of transgressors is hard;* and truly such as travel in that way, not only forsake their own mercies, but multiply their miseries at every step. Be not deceived with appearances. While men are so jovial in their revels, how often, even when the face is gay, is the heart sad! Colonel Gardiner, while he was eagerly pursuing the vanities and follies of the world, appeared always so full of life and spirit, that he got the name of the *happy rake*; but, after he became a new man, he declared, that, at the very time when he seemed so merry that others envied his pleasures, he was often so miserable in his own mind, as to wish himself a dog! It was a saying of Augustine, "The pleasures of sin are momentary; but its punishments are eternal." These pleasures, even while they last, are mixed with bitterness.

I grant that there are some, who seem so completely stupefied, as not in the least to feel their wretchedness. But a time is coming, that will awake them from sleep, and put all their dreams to flight. Hear the prosperous worldling saying to himself,

CHAPTER 1: ON THE STATE OF THE IMPENITENT

> *Soul, thou has much goods laid up for many years; take thine ease; eat, drink, and be merry. Luke 12:19.*

But hold, vain boaster! those goods are not thy own. He who lent them, has not given up His right, nor forgotten His claim. Those many years set down in thy reckoning, are not written in the book of God's decrees. Hark! a messenger knocks at the door. *This night thy soul is required of thee!* Instead of taking thy ease, now go take thy trial. Amidst all the stores prepared for the perishing body, what provision hast thou for the immortal soul? Alas, poor wretch! thou hast had no shelter for it, but a refuge of lies; no clothing, but filthy rags; no food but empty husks.* (*Boston's Fourfold State.) O miserable condition, for the soul to be hurried unpardoned, unpurified, and unprepared, into the presence of a righteous and all-seeing Judge!

THE PROMOTION OF SELF-EXAMINATION AND HUMILITY

If such as has just been described is the state of the impenitent, let me entreat you, reader, to examine whether it be your present condition.

> *If we say we have no sin, we deceive ourselves, and the truth is not in us. (1 John 1:8).*

And believe me, there is no kind of deception, into which you are so likely to fall, and which is so dangerous, as self-deception. When you are warned against it, do not imagine the caution is unnecessary. A well-known writer has justly observed, "That it is as easy to deceive ourselves without perceiving it, as it is difficult to deceive others without its being perceived." Consider what Christ says to the church at Laodicea:

> *Because thou sayest, I am rich, and increased with goods, and have need of nothing; and knowest not*

REPENTANCE EXPLAINED AND ENFORCED

> *that thou art wretched, and miserable, and poor, and blind, and naked: (Revelation 3:17).*

Do you desire to know how it is that men deceive themselves, as to their own state?

They call things by false names, and dress them in false colors.

Sin, though in itself black as hell, is whitened over with fine words and fair pleas. The most extravagant and mischievous outrages are softly termed the frolics of youth. Vain conversation, bubbling into frothy levity, or breaking out into filthy lewdness, is called harmless mirth. A compliance with idle fashions and dangerous amusements, is called seeing and knowing the world. Drinking, gaming, swearing, and Sabbath-breaking are a *gay life*. On the other hand, pious men are named sour bigots, or sly hypocrites. Religion is termed a melancholy thing; and a strict regard to it, madness.

> *Woe unto them that call evil good, and good evil; that put darkness for light, and light for darkness; that put bitter for sweet, and sweet for bitter! (Isaiah 5:20).*

Beware you do not fall under this woe. Let every disguise be torn away. Be willing to know the worst of yourself, that you may avoid delusion. I dare say you do not wholly deny your sin; but do you not spare it, and half excuse it? Perhaps your confession runs in such language as this: "I have been *rather* thoughtless, a *little* too wild; but I always intended to reform." Or it may be, you compare yourself with others, and begin to sound the Pharisee's trumpet, saying, "I am no extortioner, adulterer, nor drunkard; I have never gone the lengths that many have done; I do no one any harm; and if I be not safe, what will become of thousands?" Now, be persuaded to examine yourself by the light of God's holy law. Do not talk of what *other* men *are*, but of what *you ought to be*. Labor to gain a full view of the holiness and majesty of God; and

CHAPTER 1: ON THE STATE OF THE IMPENITENT

then you will clearly perceive the infinite evil of sin, and your own depravity as a sinner. While a garment is kept in the dark, its filthiness is not seen; but bring it to the light, and every spot becomes visible.

Many are deceived as to their own state, because they are strangers to the heart.

If they keep free from gross vices and shocking crimes; if they are sober in their appetites, and honest in their dealings; if they behave decently towards their superiors, and attend constantly on public worship; they think themselves very good characters. They are whole, and need not a physician; safe, and look not for a Savior.

> *The heart is deceitful above all things, and desperately wicked, who can know it? (Jeremiah 17:9).*

Does not the experience of every day confirm these words of the prophet? What maze has such windings, what cavern has such dark retreats, what whirlpool has such dangerous deeps and violent motions, as the human heart? It is bad to have an enemy anywhere; it is worse to have one preparing schemes of mischief in your own house; but it is worst of all, to have a secret, plotting, and active working foe, within your own bosom. Though you may not be a base liar, a bold blasphemer, a beastly drunkard, or an impious scoffer; if the heart be not right with God, all must be wrong. Now look within, and see. Do not take this matter upon trust, but upon trial. I venture to declare, you will find every dark chamber of the heart, full of idols and abominations. Take the word of God as your light, and pray for the Holy Spirit as your guide, that you may examine those regions of the world within, to which you have been a stranger. Look into the imagination, and see what swarms of vain and sinful thoughts are there. Look into the understanding, and see what errors, prejudices, and delusions are there. Look into the conscience, and see what records of long forgotten sins, which must soon be read

REPENTANCE EXPLAINED AND ENFORCED

against you, are preserved there. Look into the affections, and see what storms of anger, fumes of pride, and flames of lust, rise there. A little time spent in close self-examination may do you more good than reading a thousand books. Sometimes an instance, or a fact drawn from life, may not only bring with it great evidence, but also fix the attention and fasten on the memory. A few years ago, two pious weavers were conversing together, and complaining of the trouble which they found from vain and evil thoughts, in the solemn duties of religion. Another person of the same business overheard them, and rushing forth said, "I always thought you two vile hypocrites, but now I know it from your own confession. For my part, I never had such vain and wicked thoughts in my life." One of the men took a piece of money out of his pocket, and put it into his hand, adding, "this shall be yours, if after you come from church next time, you can say you had not one vain thought there." In a few days he came saying, "here, take back your money, for I had not been five minutes in the church, before I began to think how many looms could be set up in it." It is for want of watching over the heart with godly jealousy, that so many are insensible of their sins. We see myriads of motes in a room when the sun shines, not one of which was beheld before.

If such as has now been described, is our condition, what cause have we for deep humiliation.

> *Thus saith the Lord, I had planted thee a noble vine, wholly a right seed: how then art thou turned into the degenerate plant of a strange vine unto me?"* (Jeremiah 2:21)

Lord, what is man! where shall we find the fruits of righteousness in their season? Where now are holy love, cheerful resignation, and perfect obedience? Ah! it is mercy that has spared, year after year, the cumberer of the ground, for justice might have cut it down, and cast it into the fire.

CHAPTER 1: ON THE STATE OF THE IMPENITENT

God made man upright; but they have sought out many inventions. Where is the image of God, which consisted in knowledge and true holiness? Where is the glory which adorned the soul as it came out of the hands of its Maker? Lord, what is man! How is the gold become dim! How is the most-fine gold changed? in place of the divine image, are seen the black marks of iniquity.

Could you enter a temple in ruins, without melancholy thoughts? Would you not say, how are beauty and grandeur turned into desolation? The lamps are extinguished; the altar is overturned; *the glory is departed!* And was not man made to be a temple for God? At first the light of truth shone in his understanding; the language of praise flowed from his lips. *Lord, what is man!* How is the temple become a den of thieves! Where now is Paradise, with its blooming beauties, and sacred sweets? Speak to the earth, and it shall teach thee a lesson in humility. Where canst thou turn thine eye, or set thy foot, without finding proofs of thy depravity?

> *Cursed is the ground for thy sake! Thorns also and thistles shall it bring forth to thee.* (Genesis 3:17 and 18).

What are the pains which pierce the body, but the poisoned darts of sin? What are all the terrors of death, but the fruits of sin? Sin opened the sluices of divine wrath, and let into the world those floods of misery, which have spread their bitter waters over every land! Well, then, may we humble ourselves under the mighty hand of God, and cry, Lord,

> *What is man, that thou art mindful of him, or the son of man, that thou visitest him?*

CHAPTER 2
ON THE NATURE OF REPENTANCE

In the last chapter, I proved that all are by nature in a state of spiritual darkness and distance from God, defiled with sin and exposed to future punishment. It is no easy matter to believe a doctrine, so grating to all the feelings with self-love fondly cherishes. Yet this is necessary, as a first step in religion; and without it, we stumble at the threshold. Having opened the way, I shall now proceed to show the nature of repentance. It is of the highest importance that we should have right sentiments on this subject. There are few persons but sometimes hear or speak of repentance. The vilest reprobates will, in their more sober moments, own the need of repentance. While men are in the very act of sinning against God, the mind is now and then struck with a thought of repentance. But we have reason to fear, there are not many who have just ideas of what the scriptures mean by this term. Some take the name for the thing, the shadow for the substance. Others think of nothing better that a slight reformation. If the wound be skinned over, they conclude it is healed. If the wild beast be chained, they are not concerned that it should be tamed. What numbers are there, who vainly imagine they have a power to produce the change required in themselves. Strangers to the corruption of the heart, and the strength of evil habits, they suppose they can forsake vice and become virtuous when they please, and *leap out of Delilah's lap into Abraham's bosom*. Sin first deceives, next stupefies, and at last destroys. While men entertain such loose, erroneous notions, trusting to their own power, and despising or neglecting the grace of God, it may be truly said, they put their repentance in the place of Christ. It is necessary therefore that we should carefully guard against every thing which leads to such delusions.

CHAPTER 2: ON THE NATURE OF REPENTANCE

I shall endeavor first to show,

THE NATURE OF TRUE REPENTANCE

That repentance which issues in life eternal, is a change of mind, contrition of heart, and deep self-abhorrence.

A SINCERE PENITENT HAS A CHANGE OF MIND

While a sinner is in a carnal state, his views and sentiments, his hopes and fears, his aims and motives, are directly contrary to what they ought to be. He scorns substantial blessings, and catches at shadows. He refuses the heavenly manna, and according to the language of the prophet, feeds upon ashes. He rejects the pearl of great price, and rakes up despicable rubbish. The things of the spirit of God, in which alone there is true wisdom, appear foolishness to him. As his imagination gilds every thing with false colors, he is pleased where he should be disgusted, and disgusted where he ought to be please. He is like a hungry man that dreameth, and behold he eateth, but he awaketh and his soul is empty; or a thirst man that dreameth, and behold he drinketh, but he awaketh and he is faint. Isaiah 29:8.

But in repentance, a happy change takes place. He who is brought under the saving influence of divine grace, is renewed in the spirit of his mind. The eyes of his understanding are enlightened, to see the vanity of the world, the evil of sin, and the value of eternal possessions. Whatever relates to God, to Christ, and to the immortal soul, now appears in a new light.

A Sincere Penitent has Right Views of God

Once he did not like to retain God in his knowledge. He had a revolting and a rebellious heart. The law of God, requiring perfect obedience, was thought too strict. The justice of God, preparing a cup of indignation for the

REPENTANCE EXPLAINED AND ENFORCED

wicked, was thought too severe. The worship of God, was felt to be a weariness and an intolerable burden.

While such was the frame of the sinner's mind, no wonder he should turn away from religion with hatred and scorn. Job describes the wicked in prosperity, in the following remarkable language:

> Therefore they say unto God, Depart from us; for we desire not the knowledge of thy ways. What is the Almighty, that we should serve him? and what profit should we have, if we pray unto him? (Job 21:14 and 15).

One of this character hates the light, because his deeds are evil. But he who has undergone a thorough change, has new thoughts of God. He sees that he is supremely great, and infinitely gracious, worthy of the highest love and reverence, from every creature in earth and heaven. He is convinced, that the law is holy, just, and good, and even when it condemns himself, goes not a jot too far. He is ready to own, that if he had been compelled to drink the cup of wrath, and wring out its bitterest dregs, he should not have had a drop more than he deserved. In short, he perceives that God is a rock, his work is perfect, his word is pure, and all his ways are wonderful, and past finding out. And is it not evident, that the more the holiness and goodness of the Lord are seen, the blacker and viler sin will appear? "The carnal man," as a good writer observes, "is apt to think God ought to repent of making such hard laws, rather than that he himself should repent of breaking them." Instead of changing his course, and turning out of the broad into the narrow way, he acts as if God would change his councils, and give blessings where he has threatened curses. Now every true penitent has quite different views. He honors God, and abases himself in the dust. Far from fretting and murmuring against the Lord, he stands amazed at his longsuffering.

CHAPTER 2: ON THE NATURE OF REPENTANCE

A Sincere Penitent has Right Views and New Thoughts of Christ

Once Jesus appeared to him as a root out of dry ground, having no form or comeliness, to make him desired. But now his divine excellency and glory are discerned and acknowledged. He bows himself at the feet of Jesus, and looks to him as the great Shepherd, Surety, Savior, and Redeemer of his people. He beholds the brightness of the Father's glory, the express image of his person, and the fullness of the Godhead in Christ. He sees all the promises and provisions of the gospel, as well as the keys of death and hell, in the mighty and faithful hands of Christ. What words can truly set forth the astonishing condescension and kindness of the Savior? "If," said Austin, "the whole sea were ink, and every blade of grass a pen, we could not fully describe the love of Christ." It is impossible to have clear views, or spiritual discoveries of the adorable Redeemer, and not to be in a considerable degree affected by them. Mr. Flavel calls repentance the tear that drops from the eye of faith, while looking to Jesus. Who can behold the Son of God coming in the flesh, laying down his life as a sacrifice, and conquering death and the powers of darkness for us, without feeling a glow of love to him? *To them that believe he is precious.*

A Sincere Penitent has New Thoughts of His Own Soul

Once the boy engaged all his care. That it might be adorned and admired, pleased and pampered, he spared no pains or costs. *What shall I eat, what shall I drink, and wherewith shall I be clothed?* if not the cry of his lips, was the language of his heart. But now being enlightened from above, he beholds the unspeakable worth of the immortal soul, and his chief concern is its salvation. O, says he, I have played the fool, and erred exceedingly in providing for the flesh, and neglecting the better part – the never dying spirit! How shall I be delivered from the wrath to come? *What shall I do to be saved?* If my house were burnt

REPENTANCE EXPLAINED AND ENFORCED

down, I might get another; if my friends were cut off, I might procure new ones; if my health were destroyed, it might be restored; but if my soul be lost, it can never be recovered, and will be utterly undone. Such are the views of a true penitent!

And let me ask, are your thoughts of God, of Christ, and of your own soul, very different from what they once were? Without such a change of mind, there cannot be genuine repentance.

> *Therefore if any man be in Christ, he is a new creature: old things are passed away; behold, all things are become new.* (2 Corinthians 5:17).

I do not say that repentance is always produced by the same means, or in the same manner. In one instance, the mind is changed, as a river gradually drawn into a fresh channel; and in another, as a river turned into a new course, by the shock of an earthquake. Such was the difference between the conversion of Saul of Tarsus, and that of Lydia.

REPENTANCE IS CONTRITION OF HEART

The prophets of old called the Jews a stiff-necked, stout-hearted, and rebellious people. How many in the present day answer to this description! Though we warn them, admonish them, entreat them, and thunder aloud in their ears the threatenings of the law; though we show them the nearness of death, the certainty and solemnity of the last judgement, the transporting happiness of heaven, and the endless, unutterable misery of hell – they remain unaffected and unconcerned! They sleep like Jonah! while the tempest, which their own sins have raised, threatens them with instant destruction. How awful is it to see this daring presumption, the unfeeling stupidity, continued to the last hour of life! "There are some persons," says Mr. Simpson, "so hardened in sin, and so totally given up of God, that neither sickness nor death can make any

CHAPTER 2: ON THE NATURE OF REPENTANCE

impression on them." He mentions one of this unhappy description in Essex, not far from the place where I now write; whom he both visited during his illness, and interred after he was dead. He was of a good family, and possessed good abilities; but wasted all his property and ruined his constitution, in a course of riot and excess. Among his bottle companions, he made a jest of hell, and turned everything sacred into ridicule. In this way he lived, and died a martyr to spirituous liquors; cursing and blaspheming to the last, notwithstanding all that could be done to bring him to a better mind.* (* Simpson's Plea for Religion, p. 256) O the blinding and hardening nature of sin!

What poison is so subtle, so dangerous, so deadly? How does it brutalize and ruin the soul! How does it warp the judgment, pervert the will, and stupefy the heart!

If you work all uncleanness with greediness, you will in a short time be past feeling. Reproofs will have no edge to wound; warnings, no weight to move you. And is there any thing on earth more to be dreaded than such a state? There is truth in the saying of a good author, "It is better to have a burdened conscience than a benumbed conscience; you had better be overfearful, than have no fear of God before your eyes." The words of the apostle to the Hebrews are never out of season:

> But exhort one another daily, while it is called To day; lest any of you be hardened through the deceitfulness of sin. (Hebrews 3:13).

True Repentance is a State of Mind

Now, true repentance is a state of mind, directly opposite to that which I have just described. It is in the scriptures called *a broken heart* or *a contrite spirit. (Psalm 51:17). The sacrifices of God are a broken spirit: a broken and a contrite heart, O God, thou wilt not despise.* Men, as one observes, despise broken things; but God does not

REPENTANCE EXPLAINED AND ENFORCED

despise a broken heart; so far from it, that he accounts the sorrow of a penitent sinner more valuable than the most costly sacrifice. When the word of God is applied by the power of divine grace, the flinty heart melts into tender grief, and the eyes overflow with floods of tears. What anxious thoughts! what strong and cutting convictions are now felt! When the fountains of the great deep are broken up within, what agonies wring the soul! O, says the sinner, I have rebelled against God whom angels adore! I have broken his laws, defied his judgments, and despised his mercies. I have neglected the great salvation, and ungratefully slighted that compassionate and glorious Redeemer, who gave his life a ransom for me! I have turned a deaf ear to the joyful sound of the gospel, and done despite unto the Spirit of Grace! Such things as these are the arrows of the Almighty, which pierce the heart with the keenest anguish, and make those deep wounds, which nothing but the balm of Gilead can heal. What is pain of body, compared with distress of mind? The spirit of a man will sustain his infirmity, but a wounded spirit who can bear? Yet we may truly say, he who thus sincerely mourns over his sins, shall not eternally sink under them.

Behold David, that broken-hearted penitent. How deeply he laments his sin. How fully and feelingly he confesses it. How humbly and earnestly he prays for pardoning and renewing grace.

> *For I acknowledge my transgressions: and my sin is ever before me. Against thee, thee only, have I sinned, and done this evil in thy sight: Purge me with hyssop, and I shall be clean: wash me, and I shall be whiter than snow. Make me to hear joy and gladness; that the bones which thou hast broken may rejoice. (Psalm 51:4, 7 and 8).*

He did not cast a hasty glance at sin, and soon forget it again. No; wherever he went, it seemed to haunt him as a frightful monster. It was not the injury done to men, so

CHAPTER 2: ON THE NATURE OF REPENTANCE

much as the offensiveness of his crimes to God that filled him with bitterness. There are few, who do not sometimes feel a pang of remorse; but the contrition of David's heart is compared to the anguish of broken bones.

Behold the penitent publican, mentioned in Luke 18:13. Pressed beneath the load of his guilt, he goes to the temple to pray.

> *And the publican, standing afar off, would not lift up so much as his eyes unto heaven, but smote upon his breast, saying, God be merciful to me a sinner.*

His distance, and humble posture, betoken the sense he felt of his own unworthiness, conscious that he might have been, in justice, everlastingly banished from the holy temple, and all the means of grace. His smiting upon his heart, silently, but expressly said, here lies my guilt, my greatest burden; here are deep fixed the barbed and bitter arrows of remorse. His short, but solemn and fervent prayer, flew up to heaven, and speedily brought down pardon, so he went down to his house justified. Do not think his case was a singular one. While you remain on earth, you will need daily to put up the same petition to God. That excellent man, Archbishop Usher, often said he hope to die with the language of the publican in his mouth, and he who wrote his life, tells us, his wish was fulfilled; he died saying, God be merciful to me, a sinner.

Behold the penitent prostitute in Luke 7:37. She goes uncalled into the house of Simon the Pharisee, to carry her broken heart, and her box of ointment, to Jesus. Had she continued in her old course of sin, instead of seeking Christ, she would have shunned him, saying with the devils, art thou come to torment me? But now, as Bishop Hall observes, "those eyes which had been fires of lust, are become fountains of tears; and those hairs which had been nets to catch her wanton lovers, are made a towel to wipe her Redeemer's feet." And though Simon murmured, the meek and merciful Savior said, her sins,

REPENTANCE EXPLAINED AND ENFORCED

which are many, are forgiven her. In the last two instances, humility and penitence are set in a more striking light, by being opposed to the disgusting pride, presumption, and un-charitableness of the self-righteous Pharisees.

I might easily produce many more examples, but I shall only mention one. Hear the confession of that well known penitent, the Earl of Rochester, who had been a worthless profligate. On his death-bed he cried out, "O blessed God, can such a horrid creature as I am be accepted by thee, who have denied thy being, and contemned thy power? Can there be mercy and pardon for me? Will God own such a wretch as I?" In the midst of his sickness, he said still farther: "Shall the unspeakable joys of heaven be conferred upon me? O, mighty Savior, never, but through thine infinite love and satisfaction! O, never, but by the purchase of thy blood!" adding, that with all abhorrence he reflected upon his former life, that from his heart he repented of all that folly and madness, of which he had been guilty.

And now, reader, ask yourself, as in the sight of God, whether you know any thing of this godly sorrow. Has your heart been touched and dissolved by the goodness of God? Have you, like David, cast your soul at the footstool of Jehovah? Have you smitten your guilty bosom like the publican? Have you sighed and wept over your transgressions, and prayed, as in an agony, for pardon and peace? Be assured, repentance is no such light thing as many have supposed. The bars of unbelief and prejudice must be broken, and the heart of stone turned into a heart of flesh. Think not a few words of confession, or drops of grief, are all that is required. The conscience once softened, must never lose its tenderness. Till we cease from sinning, the stream of repentance must not cease from flowing. "Tears," said Bishop Hopkins, "are the inheritance of our eyes," either our sufferings call for them,

CHAPTER 2: ON THE NATURE OF REPENTANCE

or our sins; and nothing can wholly dry them up, but the dust of the grave.

REPENTANCE IS DEEP SELF-ABHORRENCE

When the covetous and wretched Achan, who was a troubler of Israel, was drawn by lot, Joshua said unto him,

> My son, give, I pray thee, glory to the LORD God of Israel, and make confession unto him; and tell me now what thou hast done; hide it not from me. (Joshua 7:19).

It is no easy thing to bring down the proud looks and high thoughts of vain man. Very few are willing to give glory to God, and take shame to themselves. No sooner, however, does a man come to his right mind, that his self-flattering notions vanish. Instead of boasting, he lays his hand upon his mouth, and bows his soul to the dust, before the most high God. While he views his sins, he is abased and confounded, with a consideration of their number, their greatness, and their fruits.

The penitent is abased and confounded with,

A View of the Number of His Sins

He looks back, and sees what negligence, ingratitude, and rebellion have run through the years of past life. He looks within, and sees legions of vain thoughts, thick as motes in the sun, and shoals of hateful lust and vicious passions, working as in a troubled sea. He finds he has been adding folly to folly, and sin to sin, till his guilt rises as a mountain, and shuts out the prospect of heaven. He owns that the corruption of his nature has been pouring forth, without ceasing, streams of actual transgression and abomination, from the beginning of life to the present moment. How sincerely then can he adopt the words of the Psalmist,

> Mine iniquities have taken hold upon me, so that I am not able to look up; they are more than the hairs

of mine head: therefore my heart faileth me. (Psalm 40:12).

Do you exclaim, it is not so with me? Perhaps you fix your thoughts on two or three glaring crimes, and overlooking the rest, think your sins are but few. To remove your error, let me desire you to consider, for a moment, the sins of the tongue only. Even in this little member you will find a world of iniquity. Not only for every oath, and every lie, but also for every idle word, men must give account to God. And "if," as the pious Bishop Beveridge observes, "all our vain and idle words had been written, how many vast volumes would they make!" Who then can number the millions and millions of his sins, in thought, speech and conduct? It is well for us, that the free gift is of *many* offences unto justification of life. However great the sum of our transgression, the multitude of God's mercies is still greater. Though the catalogue of our sins were long enough to reach from earth to heaven, the ample roll of new covenant blessings would stretch beyond it. *Where sin abounded, grace does much more abound.*

The penitent is abased and confounded with,

A View of the Greatness of His Sins

We must not be guided by the prevailing loose opinions of the world. The worst men have generally the least sense of the heinousness or evil of sin. If the prisoner, who is tried for his crimes, were to fix the measure of his guilt, rather than the judge set to enforce the laws, who would be condemned or punished? Now let it be remembered, every sin is blame-worthy, just in the degree that it opposes the truth, holiness, and goodness of God. Suppose you saw a man go to a just and amiable prince, and begin to revile him in abusive language, spit in his face out of contempt, and strike him with malice, would you not think such conduct highly blamable? But should you be told, that the same person had received from the prince,

CHAPTER 2: ON THE NATURE OF REPENTANCE

whom he so reviled and injured, a thousand favors, would you not call him a monster of ingratitude and wickedness? And let it be considered, that God is the glorious King of kings, your creator and preserver, who has all your life loaded you with benefits. Every wicked deed, every profane word, and every vile thought, casts contempt upon the Majesty of heaven. The bold transgressor is up in arms of rebellion against God, and is continually either striking at his authority, or trampling on his goodness. Who then can describe the horrid nature and heinous evil of sin? The infinitely holy and glorious Jehovah himself says,

> O do not that abominable thing which my soul hateth! He has given us his law, that sin, by the commandment, might appear exceedingly sinful. (Romans 7:13).

When a true penitent has a full view of the evil and odiousness of sin, he cannot but lie abased before God. He takes up as his own, the words of Job, *Lo! I abhor myself, and repent in dust and ashes*. He can heartily join with Ezra and say,

> O my God, I am ashamed and blush to lift up my face to thee, my God: for our iniquities are increased over our head, and our trespass is grown up unto the heavens. (Ezra 9:6).

When I look at thy mercies, I am confounded and covered with shame. What tender calls and solemn admonitions have I neglected! What early and abundant advantages have I lost! What precious privileges and opportunities have I despised! If I look to the beasts, they reproach me, and cover me with shame and confusion.

> *The ox knoweth his owner, and the ass his master's crib: but Israel doth not know, my people doth not consider. (Isaiah 1:3).*

REPENTANCE EXPLAINED AND ENFORCED

Surely my sin is written as with a pen of iron, or the point of a diamond, and nothing but the blood of Christ can blot it out.

The penitent is abased and confounded with,

A View of the Fruits and Effects of His Sins

God declares, that the wicked shall eat the fruit of his own doings. Now as there is bitterness in every drop of gall, and in every branch of wormwood, so there is misery in every sin. The man who is brought to true repentance, will freely acknowledge this. Ask him, *What fruit have you in those things whereof you are now ashamed?* He replies, bitter fruit indeed! I dishonored and offended my God, wronged and ruined my own soul, encouraged and emboldened my friends and neighbors in their evil ways! *O that my head were waters, and mine eyes a fountain of tears, that I might weep day and night for my sins!* The fire which I could easily kindle, I cannot quench. The bad seed I have sown has already taken root, and spreads against all my endeavors to prevent it. Much of the evil I have done, can never be undone. O, my God, if thou art reconciled to me, how can I be reconciled to myself? Even the riches of thy free forgiving grace only show me, in a clearer light my own utter unworthiness and vile depravity.

Do you think these expressions of self-abhorrence too strong? Do you cry out, this is carrying the thing too far? Let it however be settled whether it be so or not, by an appeal to the scriptures. If what has been said be not agreeable to them, let it be condemned and rejected. Hear what the Lord says to Israel by the prophet Ezekiel,

> And there shall ye remember your ways, and all your doings, wherein ye have been defiled; and ye shall lothe yourselves in your own sight for all your evils that ye have committed. (Ezekiel 20:43).

It is not possible to use stronger expressions than these. And as we live amidst greater light, can it be

CHAPTER 2: ON THE NATURE OF REPENTANCE

supposed that our sins are less hateful, and less hurtful than those of the ancient Jews? It appears also from other parts of the same prophecies, that this kind of silent, soul-softening grief and humiliation, is necessary even when God declares himself pacified towards us. Ezekiel 16:63. There is nothing in the world can cast down self-love, and stir up self-loathing, like a believing regard to a pardoning God, and a sin-atoning Savior.

Having shown the nature of repentance, I shall conclude this chapter with a few needful cautions.

NEEDFUL CAUTIONS CONCERNING TRUE REPENTANCE

Do not Put Confession of Sin in the Place of Repentance

I grant, indeed, we ought to confess with our mouths, as well as believe with our hearts. An humble soul is ready to join with David, *For I will declare mine iniquity; I will be sorry for my sin. (Psalm 38:18)*; but these two do not always go together. It is probable you have often united with others in saying, *O Lord, we have offended against thy holy laws; we have left undone those things which we ought to have done, and have done those things which we ought not to have done*. Have not those words passed through your lips, without one serious thought ever passing through your mind? You have hundreds of times declared yourself one among miserable sinners, and yet perhaps never truly felt your misery. Shall I say such confessions are empty, unmeaning sounds? a mere waste of breath? This would be even saying too little; for when careless and impious men utter such things, it is downright hypocrisy. *Be not deceived; God is not mocked*. Is it not shocking to think of men pouring out prayers one hour, and belching out horrid oaths the next? Doth a fountain send forth at the same time sweet water and bitter? The Pharisees made long prayers in the synagogues and in the streets, to be seen of men, not to be heard of God. I have read of Romish priests teaching their blind and bigoted followers, that one confession in a year, if well paid for, would prevail with Peter to open the gates of heaven. Others have taken care to repeat a certain number of prayers every day, as regularly as the clock strikes, and made this the ground of their hope. Can you think the great God is pleased with mere lip-service and formality? No, if you were to condemn yourself in the most abasing language, and sit down in sackcloth and ashes, all this would avail nothing, while the heart remained unaffected and un-humbled.

Do not Mistake the Occasional Meltings of Natural Affection, for Repentance

Some, from their constitution, are more soft and yielding than others. When a sermon is warmly addressed to the passions, they dissolve into tears. When a death takes place in their family, they weep and seem much affected; but in a very short time it is all gone. Their tears are scarcely dried up, before they return to their former follies. Their goodness is like the morning cloud or the early dew. Yet is not this natural tenderness often mistaken for real repentance? Beware that you are not so deceived. If you are possessed of soft and lively feelings, this caution is highly necessary. You many hear of death, and resemble a man starting from his sleep, who almost instantly falls back upon his pillow, and is never quite awake. You may hear of your sins, and make confession, but never hate them or abhor yourself for committing them. You may read the mournful history of a Savior's sufferings, and weep just as you would over any other moving story. Such feelings as these are no sure signs of repentance. Ice may be a little thawed on the surface, while the warm sun-beams dart upon it, and yet be soon, frozen again as hard as a stone. A poet observes, "that tears rise from different causes, as if from separate cisterns in the soul." There is but one spring from which evangelical repentance can flow,

CHAPTER 2: ON THE NATURE OF REPENTANCE

and that spring, which is in a state of nature shut up and sealed, can be opened by none but the Holy Spirit. When his power touches the heart, as the rod of Moses smote the rock, the waters gush out, and continue to run through the whole wilderness. Doubtless a man may mourn and murmur, but never come to a right mind. See the worn-out reprobate. He repents, of what? not that he has sinned against God, but that his fortune is squandered, his family ruined, his health destroyed. His will is the same, if he had but the means to pursue his old ways. Esau cried earnestly, and wept bitterly, when he sought his father's blessing; and yet he was a profane person; there was not a drop of godly sorrow in all his tears. (Hebrews 12:16).

When You Begin to Feel Some Serious Concern, be not Eager to Get Rid of Your Uneasiness by Improper Means

Too many try to banish their fears, and bury their convictions, amidst the tumults and cares of the world. This is sure to make what is bad, still worse. If you banish your fears, they will return as an armed host, increased both in number and force. If you bury your convictions, they will most likely soon rise again, and haunt you in every place. When Felix sent for Paul, to hear him concerning the faith in Christ, it was perhaps to gratify his curious humor. But while Paul reasoned of righteousness, temperance, and judgment to come, Felix trembled. A very remarkable instance of the power of conscience! It is common enough for prisoners to tremble at the sight of the judge; but it was a new thing for a judge to tremble at the words of a prisoner. It would have been a favorable sign, had the governor cried, O Paul! these are the weightiest things I have ever heard in my life. Open and explain to me these doctrines at large. There is no time to be lost. If there is a judgment to come, how shall I give up my account? How can I be pardoned and accepted? Unhappy Felix! instead of taking this method, he said, *Go thy way for this time, and when I have a more convenient season I will send for thee.*

REPENTANCE EXPLAINED AND ENFORCED

Many, says an old divine, are glad to get rid of the shaking ague, thought it should leave them in a deep decline. While Paul was relating his own conversion, Agrippa cried, *Almost thou persuades me to be a Christian*. O, beware you do not act over again the foolish part of Felix, and the timid halting of Agrippa. If you flee from the avenger of blood, and stop short, though but a few steps from the refuge, you will be assuredly apprehended and punished. O, do not trifle with eternal things, or labor to smother those convictions which sometimes seize the conscience. Do not throw down the book which makes you uneasy, or shun the face of a faithful reprove. It is to avoid present pain, that many rush into eternal punishment. To imagine you can gain ease, by mixing with the giddy multitude, is quite as absurd as to think of healing a wound by laying on a plaister, before the thorn is removed.

Do not rest content with what the world calls morality

This too often put in the place of repentance. Many build up a wall, and daub it with untampered mortar; and because it looks well, conclude all is safe. Ezekiel 13:10 and 11. But as the materials are bad, and the foundation sandy, however it may be plastered and adorned, when the sapping rains descend and the violent winds blow, it will fall, and bury the foolish builders under its ruins. If you seem troubled about your sins, and the prospect of future misery, false teachers will tell you to live a good life and make yourself quite easy. But the apostles always directed sensible, inquiring sinners, at once to Christ. You have no hope left you, but what is centered in Christ. You must renounce your own, to trust in his righteousness. You must determine to know nothing, save Jesus Christ and him crucified. All who are forgiven, are forgiven for Christ's sake. All who are accepted, are accepted in the beloved.

He that spared not his own Son, but delivered him up for us all, how shall he not with him also freely give us all things? (Romans 8:32).

CHAPTER 2: ON THE NATURE OF REPENTANCE

But without Christ, he will bestow nothing. Do not think God will sell you eternal blessings for your poor, maimed, moral duties. *By grace are ye saved. (Ephesians 2:8)*. Neither think you will make yourself fit, and then come to Christ. If you come at all, you must come as you are. Suppose, as a good writer observes, a man to be lame and wounded; would it not be absurd to recommend him to enter the service of some great prince, to run his errands, and do his work? Ought he not first to be led to a skillful surgeon, to have his wounds cleansed and healed? Thus a sinner must be brought to repentance, before he can be trained to obedience. A moral life can flow only from a renewed heart. Elijah, says Boston, would have done the inhabitants of Jericho but little good, by purifying the bad water contained in all the vessels of their city, if he had not cast his salt into the spring. Let your constant cry be, *Lord save me, or I perish*. Plead for the forgiveness of sins and an inheritance among the saints. Pray to be justified freely, and sanctified wholly by the rich grace of our Lord Jesus Christ. Do not begin to make excuse. Now hath God granted to the Gentiles repentance unto life. May you rejoice in this grant, and live the rest of your time to him who died for you.

CHAPTER 3
ON THE NECESSITY OF REPENTANCE

It was necessary I should first tell you wherein true repentance consists. As a mistake on this point is dangerous, you ought to have right ideas of it; the most forcible addresses will otherwise be like arrows shot at random. If you are convinced that repentance is a thorough change of mind, let me entreat you to consider how *necessary* it is. When I attempt to reason with you, every page of scripture will furnish me with arguments. When I make a solemn appeal, I hope conscience will rise up as a witness within, and declare the truth, the whole truth, and nothing but the truth. When I try to persuade you, surely your own best interests should lead you to lend a willing ear, to one who has no end to answer but the promotion of your own welfare. The cause which I plead, is of infinite importance. I show you the necessity of that repentance, to which the gospel calls you. Perhaps you do not give up all thoughts of it, but determine to look to the worldly things for the present. "And what is it that thou dost count necessary? Is thy bread necessary? Is thy breath necessary? Then thy conversion is much more necessary. Indeed this is the one thing needful. Thine estate is not necessary; thou mayest sell all for the pearl of great price, and yet be a gainer by the purchase. Matthew 13:46. Thy life is not necessary; thou mayest part with it for Christ, to infinite advantage. Thy reputation is not necessary; thou mayest be reproach for the name of Christ, and yet be happy; yea, much happier in reproach than repute. 1 Peter 4:14; Matthew 5:10. But thy *conversion* is necessary." *
(* See Allein's Alarm)

I would therefore address you as Moses did Israel,

And he said unto them, Set your hearts unto all the words which I testify among you this day, which ye

CHAPTER 3: ON THE NECESSITY OF REPENTANCE

shall command your children to observe to do, all the words of this law.(Deuteronomy 32:46)

REPENTANCE IS ABSOLUTELY, UNIVERSALLY AND IMMEDIATELY NECESSARY

REPENTANCE IS ABSOLUTELY NECESSARY

Without it heaven cannot be obtained, nor hell avoided. If these can be made to appear undeniable points, other arguments can scarcely be needed for this part of the subject.

Without Repentance, It is Impossible to Obtain Heaven

Heaven is a place of pure and perfect happiness, for which there must be a suitable preparation. The apostle speaks of *being made meet to become partakers of the inheritance of the saints in light*. But to suppose there can be a fitness for heaven while you remain in a state of impenitence, is as absurd as to think a building can be finished before the first foundation-stone is laid. Every creature is suited to its own element. A fish cannot live in the air, or a bird in the water. Take a carnal man into the company of the pious, and he is miserable, because out of his own element. Accustomed to foolish and filthy talking, he has no ear for wisdom and instruction. Blinded with the glitter of vanity, he cannot discern the beauty of holiness. Feeding on dry husks and dregs of the world, he has no taste for what is pure and spiritual. He has taught his tongue to speak lies and oaths, but it has never learned to pray or praise. Sin reigns in his heart, and therefore religion has no power, nor place there. Now if such a man is wearied, and his patience worn out, by being an hour or two in the company of godly men on earth, is he not quite unfit for heaven? Were he admitted into the mansions of immortal glory, they would afford him no joy. O remember, that a heavenly temper and disposition must be brought into the soul, before the soul can be raised to heaven. We must be holy, or we cannot be happy. We must be like

REPENTANCE EXPLAINED AND ENFORCED

Christ, or we can never be with Christ. To suppose that an ungodly man can go to heaven is to suppose an impossibility. Will a father suffer a murderer to dwell among his children, or a king permit a rebel to lodge in his palace? What fellowship hath righteousness with unrighteousness? Does not Christ expressly say, *If ye believe not that I am he, ye shall die in your sins, and where I am ye cannot come*? Is not such a declaration enough to make the ears of every one that heareth to tingle? Yes, you had better, with a free pardon, die in a desert or dungeon, than with riches and honors, to die in your sins. If you be shut out from the presence of Christ, you will not have one moment of peace, one drop of comfort, or one ray of hope forever. It is a weighty maxim of Baxter, "Heaven will pay for any loss we may suffer to gain it, but nothing can pay for the loss of heaven." How strongly and solemnly is the necessity of a change of mind insisted on in the scriptures! *Jesus answered,*

> *Verily, verily, I say unto thee, Except a man be born of water and of the Spirit, he cannot enter into the kingdom of God. (John 3:5).*

If you are not washed in the laver of regeneration, and renewed by the power of the Holy Ghost, you can have no part with Christ. *Without holiness, no man shall see the Lord*. If the gospel does not change you, rest assured you impenitence will not change God's councils. False notions may lull you for a time, but they cannot turn age into youth, a bed of thorns into a bed of roses, or the king of terrors into an angel of peace.

Without Repentance, It is Impossible to Avoid Hell

Hear the faithful and true Witness – *I tell you, Nay: but, except ye repent, ye shall all likewise perish*. That the awful and weighty truth might make a deeper impression, he doubles his declaration, and by pointedly repeating the same words, applies it to the conscience with stroke upon stroke. Luke 13:3-5. To perish, in this place, does not

CHAPTER 3: ON THE NECESSITY OF REPENTANCE

mean the death of the body, for that comes alike to all, the righteous and the wicked. Nor does it mean a total loss of being, although some bad men have brought themselves to wish, and almost believe, they should die like beasts. The present life is but the porch, by which we enter into an eternal state. The Word of God assures us, *It is appointed unto men once to die, but after this the judgment.* By comparing one part of the scripture with another, we learn, that, to perish, is to be deprived of all happiness and doomed to endless misery. Peter speaks of the day of judgment and perdition of ungodly men. Christ commands us to fear him, who is able to destroy both soul and body in hell. Paul says,

> *Those who know not God, and that obey not the gospel of our Lord Jesus Christ: shall be punished with everlasting destruction from the presence of the Lord, and from the glory of his power.* (2 Thessalonians 1:8 and 9).

By examining the scriptures, you will be convinced, that to perish is for the precious soul to be irrecoverably lost! To perish is to endure indignation and wrath, tribulation and anguish, as the just punishment of sin. To perish is to be cast into outer darkness and unquenchable fire, among the workers of iniquity! What a description has our Lord given of the Dives in hell! After he had left behind him his fine linen and purple robes, he was clothed with shame and covered with confusion. Instead of those rich wines which he once drank so freely, he now begs in vain, for a drop of water to cool his tongue! O, how plainly, how positively, how solemnly, has God forewarned the wicked of eternal destruction! Can you read or hear of this without being alarmed! Can you even bear to think upon it for a moment, without terror and dismay? Do not treat these things as fancies and fables. A faithful God has stamped his threatenings, as well as his promises, with the seal of truth. Hath he said it, *and shall he not do it? Hath he spoke it, and shall he not bring it to pass? Yes, heaven and earth*

REPENTANCE EXPLAINED AND ENFORCED

shall pass away, but not one jot or tittle of his word shall be made void.

Woe to them that seek for those things only, which feed their lusts, and flatter their pride. If you remain unmelted with all the tender mercies, and unmoved with all the solemn warnings of God, how can you escape the damnation of hell? Whither will you go for shelter? What device, what contrivance do you trust to for deliverance? *Can you thunder with a voice like God? Can you wage war with the Almighty?* Can you find a corner in the vast universe, to hide you from the all-searching eyes of your Judge? When once plunged into the pit of despair, can you pass the gulf which God has fixed between heaven and hell? O, consider and believe it, there is nothing before you but repentance or ruin. Do you think it necessary to pursue your business, provide for your family, and preserve your health? These, however, are the things of time; but godliness is necessary for eternity. O, the importance of eternity! when millions of millions of years are gone, eternity will not be lessened! *The wicked*, saith *Christ, go away into everlasting punishment, and into the place prepared for the devil and his angels*. Matthew 25:46. And if, without a change, this must be your doom, is not repentance absolutely necessary? The soul is too precious to be risked for the poor trifles of a day. It is useless to gather riches and honors; for if you had whole kingdoms in your possession, they could not deliver you from death. If you continue impenitent to the last, all the angels of heaven, should they wish it, could not save you from hell. Woe unto you, if God withdraw the beams of his favor! Every creature will then forsake you. *The heavens will reveal your iniquity, and the earth shall rise up against you.* The want of penitence, after we have sinned, provokes God more than the sin itself. Has the thought of this ever yet seriously affected you? O, may you be smitten to the heart, with a conviction of your sin and danger! May you be plucked as a brand out of the burning, by the arm of

CHAPTER 3: ON THE NECESSITY OF REPENTANCE

sovereign grace! O, cry earnestly – cry unceasingly, "Lord, I have been ignorant and sensual, as a beast before thee! I have been a stubborn rebel, a hateful monster! *Turn thou me, and I shall be turned; save me, and I shall be saved*. Why am I yet spared, when thousands, less guilty, have been cut off in their sins? *Lord, enter not into judgment with thy servant; for in thy sight shall no man living be justified*. Had I been swept away into the fiery oven of thy wrath, it would have been nothing more than I have deserved. *Have mercy upon me, have mercy upon me, and blot out my sins*. Give me thy good Spirit, to soften the soil of my heart, that the incorruptible seed of truth may take root there, and bring forth an hundred fold."

REPENTANCE IS *UNIVERSALLY* NECESSARY

Do not think what has been said applies to none but blasphemers, thieves, and murderers. *All have sinned, and come short of the glory of God*. The infection has struck deep, and spread wide. Sin is a disease equally dangerous, whether it works secretly within, or breaks out into odious irruptions of vice. *Therefor God*, saith the apostle, *hath now commanded all men every where to repent*. There is not one, come to years capable of seeing the difference between good and evil, who has not sinned against God. We behold a great many different opinions, tastes, and pursuits among men: but all are transgressors, and need repentance. I shall, therefore, address myself to the profligate and presumptuous; the negligent and careless; the self-righteous and hypocritical. I address myself first,

To the Profligate and Presumptuous

It is asked, whom do I mean? I reply, do you profane the Sabbath, and spend those hours which were set apart for the service of God, in loose company, vain amusements, and vile pleasures? Do you boldly utter such wanton or indecent language, as must make a modest and good man blush? Do you give yourselves to cheating and

REPENTANCE EXPLAINED AND ENFORCED

fraud, lewdness and drunkenness? – then you are profligates. Sins of ignorance are less heinous; but these things are not only condemned by the law of God, but also contrary to the laws of men. If you practice wickedness in open daylight, against counsels, warnings, and reproofs; if you go on in your forbidden ways, willfully and obstinately, – then, you are presumptuous sinners. You can neither plead ignorance nor surprise, and therefore are left without excuse.

> Heaven from above, and
> conscience from within,
>
> Cry in your startled ears – Abstain from sin! * (* Cowper)

And yet you rush upon those rocks, against which so many have made shipwreck before your eyes! O, think, what would be your condition, if you were instantly seized by the strong hand of death! How could you appear before your Maker and Judge?

> *Know ye not that the unrighteous shall not inherit the kingdom of God? Be not deceived: neither fornicators, nor idolaters, nor adulterers, nor effeminate, nor abusers of themselves with mankind, Nor thieves, nor covetous, nor drunkards, nor revilers, nor extortioners, shall inherit the kingdom of God. (1 Corinthians 6: 9 and 10).*

Is it possible to be guilty of such things, and not know it? And can you bear any of these black marks upon your characters, and not shudder at the sight of them?

Perhaps you boast, that you never pretended to any religion. "Whatever we be, we are not canting hypocrites. We scorn the pitiful tricks of base cowards. Away with all weak scruples; we can bravely despise them; and, dashing through difficulties, enjoy our frolics, in spite of death and destruction." Let me tell you, the difference between a hypocrite and a reprobate is only like that which there is between a thief and a robber; they are both detestable.

CHAPTER 3: ON THE NECESSITY OF REPENTANCE

According the striking words of Boston, a conscience is seared as with a hot iron, is sure presage of everlasting burnings. *Who hath hardened himself against God, and prospered?* Who can raise a defense that will shield him from the flaming bolts of the Almighty?

> *For if we sin willfully after that we have received the knowledge of the truth, there remaineth no more sacrifice for sins, But a certain fearful looking for of judgment and fiery indignation, which shall devour the adversaries. (Hebrews 10:26 and 27).*

Who made Cain a fugitive and a vagabond in the earth? Genesis 4:14. Who made Pashur a terror to himself and to all his friends? Jeremiah 20:4. Who struck Belshazzar with horror, while he was feasting with his thousand lords? It was that God, to whom vengeance belongeth; who reserveth wrath for his enemies. I have read of a wicked man, who when warned of hell, said, "I will believe it when I come thither!" But what use will it be to believe there is a hell, when it is too late to escape from it? A daring and hectoring spirit cannot save you. Though you should imagine you have made a covenant with death, and with hell an agreement, so that the one shall not seize, nor the other claim you, what security can they afford? the same that you would have of an estate, held by a lease written upon the sands of the sea shore, till the coming of the next tide! When the overflowing scourge shall come, your covenant with death shall be disannulled, and your agreement with hell shall not stand. Isaiah 28:15.

Many persons, while they are full of health and spirits, make light of religion, who yet, in a time of sickness, find all their confidence fail. Mr. Hervey went to visit a man on his death bed, who had been given up to all the gaieties and pleasures of a worldly life. "I found him" (says he) "no more that sprightly son of joy, which he used to be; but languishing, pining away – withering under the chastening hand of God! His limbs feeble and trembling;

REPENTANCE EXPLAINED AND ENFORCED

his countenance forlorn and ghastly; and the little breath he had left, sobbed out in sorrowful sighs. When I was seated beside him, he first cast a most wishful look at me, and then began, as well as he was able, to speak as follows: –'O, that I had been wise; that I had known this; that I had considered my latter end! Ah! Mr. Hervey, death is knocking at my door: in a few hours more, I shall draw my last gasp; and then, judgment! tremendous judgment! How shall I appear, unprepared as I am, before the all-knowing and omnipotent God! How shall I endure the day of his coming? The day in which I should have worked is over and gone; and I see a sad, horrible night approaching, bringing with it the blackness of darkness forever! Woe is me! when he invited, I was one of them that made excuse. Now, therefore, I receive the reward of my deeds: I smart, and am in sore anguish: and yet this is but the beginning of sorrows. It doth not yet appear what I shall be; but I am sure I shall be ruined, undone, and destroyed with an everlasting destruction." It would be easy to mention many such instances. If you tread in the steps of such men, how can you expect any other than their end? *I tell you, Nay: but, except ye repent, ye shall all likewise perish*. I address myself, next,

To the Negligent and Careless

Is it asked, whom do I mean? I mean you, who lull yourselves into a false sleep; you, who glory in a settled indifference; you, who are given up to sloth, as if you had no souls to be either saved or lost.

The prophet speaks of some in his day, *who cried peace! peace! when there was no peace*. The trumpet sounded an alarm; they did not arouse, to prepare for the battle. The storm gathered black and heavy; but they persuaded themselves it would blow away, and not reach them. And do you see yourselves here described? How loud, how earnest, how frequent, how solemn have been the calls of God to you? and yet you are as senseless as

CHAPTER 3: ON THE NECESSITY OF REPENTANCE

the stones! How many awful events and judgments have passed before your eyes? and yet you remain hardened in impenitence! How many showers of goodness has God caused to descend upon you? and still you are ungrateful! Time glides away; and you neither feel remorse for the past, nor concern for the future. Death draws nearer and nearer; but you prepare not to meet your God. What! do you not know, that a messenger from heaven cries,

Woe to them that are at ease in Zion! (Amos 6:1).

Perhaps you glory in a calm, settled indifference to religion! Whatever others may think, say, or do, you determine neither to favor nor oppose it. But do you believe, that, by being careless, you shall be found guiltless? Do you really think, you can steer an even course between the righteous and the wicked? Solon made a law in Athens, that those who, in a sedition, or contest of the citizens, refused to take either part, should be esteemed infamous. It is certain, God has made a law, that, in the grand concerns of religion, no one shall stand neuter. *He that is not for us,* says Christ, *is against us*. There is no middle path between the broad and narrow way. After the gates of death are passed, there are but two final homes for all, and these are, heaven and hell! Continue, then, no longer to halt between two opinions, which are directly opposite; but *choose you whom ye will serve*. Perhaps you give yourselves to sloth; you think you are free from the crimes of the profligate. "We were never habituated to fraud, falsehood, gaming, intoxication, and profaneness. We have neither wronged the helpless, nor corrupted the innocent; neither despised governments nor mocked at religion." But though you may not be chargeable with gross, disgraceful crimes, yet, if you be estranged from God, unmindful of the gospel of Christ, and unconcerned about an eternal world, your souls are exposed to ruin.

Remember the doom of the unprofitable servant, whose talent had been suffered to rust in a napkin.

REPENTANCE EXPLAINED AND ENFORCED

Thou wicked and slothful servant, out of thine own mouth thou are condemned. And cast ye the unprofitable servant into outer darkness: there shall be weeping and gnashing of teeth. (Matthew 25: 26 and 30, Luke 19:22).

You may flatter yourselves with a false peace, and sit down in sloth and indifference: *but, except ye repent, ye shall all likewise perish.* I address myself, also,

To the Self-Righteous and Hypocritical

Is it asked, whom do I mean? I mean you, who are puffed up with the pride of self-sufficiency, and contented with a dull round of ceremonies. If regularly going to a place of worship on a Sabbath, be religion, you have been very religious from your childhood. You say your prayers every night, as constantly as a man winds up his watch, and much in the same formal and listless manner.

There are no persons, on whom the gospel has so little effect, as the self-righteous. They strike out a great variety of ways, by which to compass their end. Truth does not furnish one argument, for which their pride cannot find and objection.

For they being ignorant of God's righteousness, and going about to establish their own righteousness, have not submitted themselves unto the righteousness of God. For Christ is the end of the law for righteousness to every one that believeth. (Romans 10: 3 and 4).

Persons of this stamp will quibble away the plainest testimonies of scripture, rather than yield to become indebted to the free grace of the gospel, for justification of life. They not only err, but also fortify themselves in error. If one scheme fails, they try another. They,

that say in the pride and stoutness of heart, The bricks are fallen down, but we will build with hewn

CHAPTER 3: ON THE NECESSITY OF REPENTANCE

stones: the sycomores are cut down, but we will change them into cedars. (Isaiah 9: 9 and 10).

When Noah had entered the ark, it is emphatically said, *The LORD shut him in*. But when the self-righteous have built their own refuge, they shut themselves in, and there rest secure, till they are either driven out by the sword of the Spirit, or burnt out by the fire of divine wrath. Those cloaked hypocrites, and proud boasters, the Pharisees, were full of self-sufficiency, but looked upon all others with disdain. They scarcely thought the publicans worthy to take a place within the same walls, or walk in the path which they had made holy by their steps. Instead of trusting in the merits of the Redeemer, they hoped for acceptance with God, from their fasts, and prayers, and alms.

Are you resting your dependence on the wretched foundation of your own goodness? I must tell you, while you despise God's way, you will never be able to climb to heaven in your own way. All your virtues will not atone for one of your vices. Your scheme of religion makes void the righteousness, the sacrifice, and the grace of Jesus Christ, and therefore must assuredly fall; and if you cling to it, you must fall with it. Then, how dreadful it will be, to behold a frown of the face of the Judge, when you are expecting a welcome into the habitations of glory.

Deceitful views of future bliss, farewell!

You'll read your sentence in the flames of hell.

You are mistaken in supposing your good works will buy you a place in paradise. Christ does not save men by halves. God will not barter away eternal blessedness, for any thing that is offered by your hands. *I tell you, Nay: but, except ye repent, ye shall all likewise perish*. Your minds must be changed, and your hearts renewed, or you are utterly undone. Surely with one grain of common sense, and one ray light from above, you may know a truth

REPENTANCE EXPLAINED AND ENFORCED

so plain, as the necessity of deep repentance. What idiot is there, as one well observes, who cannot perceive the difference between a shadow and a substance? And do you mistake the form of godliness for the power of it? Can you really believe that a fine varnish will recommend a filthy vessel? Are you so stupid as to expect you shall enjoy the kernel, when you sit down contented with the empty shell? It was in vain for that false prophet, Balaam, to cry, *Let me die the death of the righteous*! Heaven was never yet gained by an idle wish! And as Balaam, at that very time, was following the wages of unrighteousness, though he uttered such fair words, he was quite as unfit for the perfect bliss of saints and angels, as the dumb ass which reproved him for his folly and madness. Think then of the holiness and majesty of God. Try yourselves by the standard of the divine law. Beware of that close lurking traitor in your own bosom, sin. Pray for the Spirit of God to show you the depths of your depravity. Every true penitent, like the poor prodigal, must first come to himself, or he will never think of coming to the Father of mercies. He must see his nakedness, and feel his wants, or he will not be clothed with the richly wrought robe of the Savior's righteousness, and welcomed to the feast of gospel blessings. He must confess and forsake his sins, or he cannot enjoy pardon and reconciliation.

REPENTANCE IS *IMMEDIATELY* NECESSARY

There is a natural disposition in all men to put far away those great concerns, which ought ever to be near their hearts. What they cannot deny to be necessary, they contrive to delay. When God sent his messages to Israel by the prophet Ezekiel, they said,

> *The vision that he seeth is for many days to come, and he prophesieth of the times that are far off. (Ezekiel 12:27).*

CHAPTER 3: ON THE NECESSITY OF REPENTANCE

And when you hear of repentance toward God, and faith towards our Lord Jesus Christ, you are probably ready to own, that they are necessary; but when? Not yet; it will be soon enough in old age; or on a death-bed. But what makes you think so? I can venture to declare, by what steps you have been led to this conclusion. You presume on a long life, on the mercy of God, and on the ground of a few examples of late repentance.

You delay repentance, by

Presuming that You shall Yet live Many Years

There was an idiot in the city of Athens, who counted all the ships that entered the port, and called them his own. Poor creature! from his want of understanding, he was to be pitied, rather than blamed. But if you confidently count those years your own, which are yet in the hand of God, you are chargeable with the grossest folly, and are without excuse. What assurance have you of a long life? Has God sealed you a lease, or sent you a promise, of thirty, twenty, or seven years to come? It may be, you are young, healthy, and vigorous, but are you sure of a single day? Do you not see innumerable diseases, vanquishing all the power of medicine? And what are these, but the forerunners and messengers of death? Do you not see your fellow creatures, of every age and rank, suddenly swept into eternity? And who knows but some fatal disease may in a few days seize your frame, or some direful accident cut you off in a moment? "We must," said Bishop Taylor, "take our water, as out of a torrent and sudden shower, which will quickly cease dropping from above, and running in our channels below." O how brittle is the tie that holds you in life! And when that slender bond is broken, you will be instantly in eternity!

> *To-day if ye will hear his voice, Harden not your hearts. (Hebrews 3:7 and 8).*

REPENTANCE EXPLAINED AND ENFORCED

Will you dare to contradict the Majesty of heaven? When God says to-day, will you say to-morrow? Will you hearken to the voice of any flatterer, rather than to the voice of your Creator, Redeemer, and Judge? If you still turn away from the faithful warnings and kind invitations of God, how justly may he swear in his wrath, that you shall not enter into his rest. You are probably very earnest and active in the things of this world, while you are so careless and dilatory concerning the world to come. Think what will be your views of such conduct in a dying hour.

That great and famed scholar Grotius, on his death-bed, spoke thus, "Ah! I have consumed my life, in a laborious doing of nothing! I would give all my learning and honor, for the plain integrity of John Urick!" This John Urick was a religious poor man, who spent eight hours of the day in reading and prayer, eight in labor, and only eight in sleep and meals. Salmatius, another learned man, when about to die, cried out bitterly against himself, saying, Oh! I have lost a world of time! time, the most precious thing in the world! If I had but one year more it should be spent in reading David's Psalms and Paul's Epistles!" "Oh," said he to his friends, "mind the world less, and God more."

And do you talk of delaying repentance to future years? The ship should be repaired before it puts to sea, for it is difficult to keep it from sinking, when the storm comes. Repent and believe, in health; sickness is not a time to begin. Are your present pleasures so highly prized, that you determine to risk the loss of the soul, rather than leave them? Have you time for every thing, except the one thing needful?

> *For what is your life? It is even a vapor, that appeareth for a little time, and then vanisheth away. (James 4:14).*

Hearken then to the serious and urgent admonition of the apostle, who introduces it with a double note of attention, to fix your thoughts upon it.

CHAPTER 3: ON THE NECESSITY OF REPENTANCE

"Behold, NOW is the accepted time; behold, NOW is the day of salvation. (2 Corinthians 6:2).

You delay repentance, by

Presuming on the Mercy of God

This I believe is a very common case. When we tell men of their sins, and point out the danger that lies before them, they cry, God is merciful, and therefore, if we repent, we shall be pardoned at last. Now I acknowledge that redeeming mercy is a most charming sound. The mercy of God reaches to the heavens. The mercy of God is the wonder of angels, and ought to be the song of mortals.

It is of the LORD'S mercies that we are not consumed, because his compassions fail not. They are new every morning: (Lamentations 3:22 and 23).

But can any thing be more base, than to make this plea to justify rebellion, and to persist in it? What would you think of a man, who, year after year, should provoke and injure his best friends, because he still hoped, through their great kindness, to be forgiven and again received into favor? But no comparison can sufficiently set forth the shameful ingratitude of those who abuse the forbearance and long-suffering of God, and continue to sin that grace may abound. Every day we may behold the truth of Solomon's words,

Because sentence against and evil work is not executed speedily, therefore the heart of the sons of men is fully set in them to do evil. (Ecclesiastes 8:11).

They take their reprieve for a release. If indeed God is long in whetting the sword of vengeance, will he never strike the fatal blow? If the storm be long gathering, will it never burst? An hundred and twenty years the patience of God waited in the days of Noah, but at the last the flood came. And do you, reader, make divine mercy a plea to encourage you in sin and presumption! Let me beg your

REPENTANCE EXPLAINED AND ENFORCED

attention to the forcible and solemn language of the apostle.

> *And thinkest thou this, O man, that judgest them that do such things, and doest the same, that thou shalt escape the judgment of God? Or despisest thou the riches of his goodness and forbearance and longsuffering; not knowing that the goodness of God leadeth thee to repentance? But after thy hardness and impenitent heart treasurest up unto thyself wrath against the day of wrath and revelation of the righteous judgment of God. (Romans 2:3-5).*

Every word in this remarkable scripture is a strong and faithful appeal to the conscience. What! do you regard small favors from men, and dare you reject or abuse the riches of God's abounding mercy? Does that goodness which should lead you to repentance, strengthen and harden you in wickedness? If you go on, perverting the gospel, and thus, as the prophet speaks, *turning blessings in curses*, what will be the consequence? The riches of divine goodness, which you now despise, will be wholly withdrawn; and the treasures of wrath, which you are laying up, will be your only and eternal portion.

You delay repentance, from

A Presumption, Built upon Remarkable Instances of *Late* Conversion

There certainly have been some awakened in the evening of their day, so late as the eleventh hour; but compared with the same number of those who die much in the same careless and hardened state in which they live, such examples are very rare. It sometimes happens, in a dreadful shipwreck, that two or three are preserved, when hundreds are buried in the deep. But, you may say, was not the penitent thief converted and pardoned on the cross? Yes, and it was both a wonderful display of infinite mercy, and an undeniable proof of the virtue of that

CHAPTER 3: ON THE NECESSITY OF REPENTANCE

precious atoning blood which Jesus was then shedding at his side. But the case of the penitent thief was singular. Life and peace entered his soul, while agony and death were racking and oppressing his body. We have one such instance, that none might despair; and but one such in the whole Bible, that none might presume. And do you hence take encouragement to give the prime of your days, and the vigor of your strength to the service of sin, and reserve only the droppings and dregs of life to the concerns of religion? After obstinately persevering for a long course of years, in rebellion against God, do you expect he will work a miracle to convert and save you in your last moments? Can you think of remaining in a state of impenitence and condemnation, till the wasted taper of life is sunk in the socket, and on the point of being extinguished by the blast of God's displeasure? And besides, there is little dependence to be placed on the religion which begins at such a time. It is a true saying of the pious Bishop Hall, "Though sincere repentance is never too late, late repentance is seldom sincere."

AN ANSWER TO TWO OBJECTIONS

Objection 1. You labor to make me worse than I am, and give a gloomy picture of misery, only to frighten me.

God forbid, that I should fancy crimes, and then fasten them on your character. I do say, that something better is necessary than the cheap outside religion, which is the trust of the proud and self-righteous. Mere decency of manners may gain you a good name among men; but real holiness of heart only, can fit you for the presence of God. Rest not, however, on my word, or the opinion of any man; but search the Word of God. It is said, there is not a just man upon the earth, that doeth good and sinneth not. Now if you are a transgressor, you need pardon. If you have departed from God, you must be converted. If heaven's pure and everlasting joys are to be desired, or

REPENTANCE EXPLAINED AND ENFORCED

hell's fiery and eternal torments are to be dreaded, repentance is absolutely necessary. Say not; this is a harsh subject. As there are some dangerous sweets, so there are some wholesome bitters. It is better you should receive truth, though it may be painful, than error mixed with the most pleasant ingredients. And besides directing you to the Word of God, I would entreat you to examine your own heart. Let the important cause be tried fully and fairly in the court of conscience. A thousand witnesses, if they may but have a hearing, will rise up within, and condemn you; and as long as you are under the law, convicted as a transgressor, the wrath of God follows you wherever you go, mingles in all you possess, and marks you as a victim devoted to destruction. *Cursed shalt thou be in the city, and cursed in the field; cursed shall be thy basket and thy store. The heavens shall reveal thine iniquity, and the earth shall rise up against thee.*

Objection 2. The severe doctrine you teach, will drive me to despair.

Although God has commanded all men everywhere to repent, many seem to think us cruel, when we insist upon it. When one vain objection after another is answered, and the awful truth brought home with many a vigorous charge upon the conscience, they lose all patience under such plain dealing. We cannot repent, say they, of ourselves, and why then urge us to it? Will it be any benefit to drive us to despair? – I do wish to make you despair of finding safety or peace in a life of sin. It would do well, did you despair of attaining heaven by your own strength, or merit, for this would be the beginning of solid hope. Luther, in one of his books, says, "God hath assuredly promised his favor to the truly humble. By the truly humble, I mean those who are endued with repentance, and a despair of saving themselves; for a man can never be said to be really penitent and humble, till he be made to know that his salvation is not suspended in any measure whatever, on

CHAPTER 3: ON THE NECESSITY OF REPENTANCE

his own strength, endeavors, free-will, or works; but entirely depends on the free pleasure and purpose of God." You can do nothing of yourself; but is the hand of the Lord shortened, that it cannot save, or his ear heavy, that it cannot hear? Your native springs are all dry; but is there not a fountain of grace, a river that makes glad the city of our God? You are as destitute and helpless as the prodigal son; but is our heavenly Father's house empty? No; in Christ, there is a never-failing fullness. Millions daily draw their supplies from it, and should millions more come, yet still there will be enough and to spare. With all my heart, I desire you may become a partaker of these blessings. It would be kind, saith one, if you saw a man trying to swim over the sea, to make him despair of an attempt so foolish, when you could lead him to a vessel ready to receive and convey him with safety. In like manner would I make you despair of happiness in the world, or help in yourself, that I may lead you to the hope of the gospel.

CHAPTER 4
ON THE MEANS OF PROMOTING REPENTANCE

VERILY, verily, I say unto you, Whosoever committeth sin is the servant of sin. (John 8:34).

This is constantly seen in the world. Every man, in his natural state, yields himself to sin. All his senses, members, and faculties, are its handmaids and ministers. The eye watches for it; the ear listens to it; the tongue pleads, and the hands toil for it! Fancy is the painter that draws its pictures; memory is the recorder that keeps its secrets; the will is its charioteer, that drives furiously through all restraints; the passions and appetites are the providers that hunt for its prey. And how can you be delivered from this hard master and all its miseries?

If the Son therefore shall make you free, ye shall be free indeed. (John 8:36).

He can loose you, and let you go; raise you, and renew your mind; but no other can. The apostle Peter told the Jews, that

The God of our fathers raised up Jesus, whom ye slew and hanged on a tree. Him hath God exalted with his right hand to be a Prince and a Savior, for to give repentance to Israel, and forgiveness of sins. (Acts 5:30 and 31).

From these words it is evident, that the change which I have proved to be absolutely necessary, is an effect flowing from the free grace of God. Man can fill the measure of his sins, but not empty it. He can plunge himself into guilt and misery; but it requires an Almighty arm to draw him out again. *O, Israel! thou hast destroyed thyself; but in me is thy help found.* Pride and self-sufficiency are some among the many proofs and effects of

CHAPTER 4: ON THE MEANS OF PROMOTING REPENTANCE

our fallen and depraved state. It has been well observed, that "the first acts of sin are like single drops of water, which, rapidly following one another, soon gather into a stream; and that stream at last swells into a torrent, and sweeps away all before it." Yet, most men, though they cannot be prevailed upon to restrain the first drops, vainly imagine they are able to stop the rolling flood. As they are not aware of the strength of sin, they think it will be an easy matter to repent, whenever they please. Dr. Preston says, "A man might as soon make, out of a clod of earth, a shining star, as turn the carnal and dead heart into the image of God!"

> *Can the Ethiopian change his skin, or the leopard his spots? then may ye also do good, that are accustomed to do evil? (Jeremiah 13:23).*

That bold blasphemer and fierce persecutor, Saul of Tarsus, was converted and pardoned! but did he ascribe the change to his own power? No! he says,

> *And the grace of our Lord was exceeding abundant with faith and love which is in Christ Jesus. This is a faithful saying, and worthy of all acceptation, that Christ Jesus came into the world to save sinners; of whom I am chief. (1 Timothy 1:14 and 15).*

The great Redeemer sends his Spirit to open the fountain of repentance in the heart. This blessing we possess in virtue of his death and intercession. It is the special office of the Holy Spirit to convince the world of sin, of righteousness, and of judgment. That true repentance flows from the grace and power of the Holy Spirit, is manifest from every part of the Old and New Testaments. It is expressed in various ways, to give us the strongest assurance of the fact. I shall now mention many passages; suffice it to produce one: –

> *And I will give them one heart, and I will put a new spirit within you: and I will take the stony heart out of*

their flesh, and will give them an heart of flesh. (Ezekiel 11:19).

"A stone, saith one, is cold, unyielding, insensible! Strike it, it resists the blow! Lay upon it a burden, it perceives no pressure! Apply a seal, it receives no impression!" Such is the heart of man, hardened in sin! But when the sweet promise, which I have just repeated, is fulfilled, this stupid senselessness gives place to tenderness.

Here it may be said, "If repentance is a gift and an effect of the Holy Spirit, how can it be a duty? why are we exhorted to repent and return to God?" To this I answer, the command of God makes it our duty; and the promise of God supplies the grace that is necessary. I should think it cruel mockery to urge you to repent, if there were no provision of mercy – no way of salvation. But there is every reason to call men to repentance, while God grants the grace of repentance, in the use of his own appointed means. Our Lord says,

> Labor not for the meat which perisheth, but for that meat which endureth unto everlasting life, which the Son of man shall give unto you. (John 6:27).

Though it is the gift of Christ, we are commanded to labor for it. In the same way do the scriptures speak of repentance, as both a duty and a privilege.

Some of the chief means which the Spirit uses for producing repentance are as follows:

THE READING OF THE HOLY SCRIPTURES, AND OTHER GOOD BOOKS

Eliphaz gives this useful advice:

Acquaint now thyself with him, and be at peace: thereby good shall come unto thee. Receive, I pray thee, the law from his mouth, and lay up his words in thine heart. (Job 22:21 and 22).

CHAPTER 4: ON THE MEANS OF PROMOTING REPENTANCE

There can be no proper knowledge of ourselves, without an acquaintance with God; and no right acquaintance with God, but by his word. The scripture is a glass in which we may see our spots and blemishes. I do not wonder that the popish priests should try to prevent the people from reading the Bible; for they wished them to remain in ignorance and stupidity. *By the law* (says Paul) *is the knowledge of sin*. It shows us both its deep roots and bitter fruits; it discovers the poisonous serpent hid among the flowers. The Word of God is *a discerner of the thoughts and intents of the heart*. "It can come, (as Gurnall says,) where no search-warrant from a magistrate can enter." When accompanied by the power of the Spirit, a thousand doors, with as many locks and bolts of prejudice and aversion, cannot hinder it from forcing a passage into the soul. It lays hold of the will, and bends it to compliance; and then, every thing else gives way. Reader! take the law of God into thy hand. How readest thou! Examine carefully every precept.

> *Thou shalt love the Lord thy God with all thy heart, and with all thy mind, and with all thy strength.*

When you fix your attention on this single command, do you not begin to falter? Have you not cause to cry out, "Alas! instead of loving the Lord with all my heart, living continually in his fear, and longing for the enjoyment of his presence, God has scarcely been in all my thoughts!"

The reading of the Holy Scriptures may be safely recommended, as a means the most suitable to produce repentance.

> *Is not my word like as a fire? Saith the LORD; and like a hammer that breaketh the rock in pieces? (Jeremiah 23:29).*

There is no metal which this fire is not able to melt and separate from dross; there is no adamant which this hammer has not force enough to break! Cyprian was

REPENTANCE EXPLAINED AND ENFORCED

converted by reading the book of Jonah! and Junius, by the first chapter of John.

Sometimes a single stroke of this hammer, a remarkable passage, directed by some particular providence, and applied by the Spirit of God, has penetrated the sinner's heart, and humbled him at the feet of Jesus.

"In Oliver Cromwell's army, every soldier had a Bible. Among the rest, there was one wild, wicked young man, who ran away from his apprenticeship in London, for the sake of plunder and dissipation. Being one day ordered out upon a skirmishing party, or to attack some fortress, he returned to his quarters in the evening without hurt. When he was going to bed, pulling the Bible out of his pocket, he observed a hole in it. He traced the depth of the hole, and found the bullet had gone as far as the eleventh chapter of Ecclesiastes, and the ninth verse:

> *Rejoice, O young man, in thy youth; and let thy heart cheer thee in the days of thy youth, and walk in the ways of thine heart, and in the sight of thine eyes: but know thou, that for all these things God will bring thee into judgment.*

The words were set home upon his heart by the Holy Spirit, so that he became a very serious believer in the Lord Jesus Christ, and used pleasantly to observe, that the Bible was the means of saving his soul and his body too."

There are many valuable books on religious subjects, which have been blessed of God as instruments for awakening thoughtless, proud, and profligate sinners. Vergerious was a violent papist, and he set about reading the protestant books on purpose to confute them; but the light broke in upon his mind, and he became a firm protestant and sincere Christian. Colonel Gardiner had a book slipped into his box by his aunt, or good mother. As the title of it was, *"Heaven Taken by Storm,"* his curiosity

CHAPTER 4: ON THE MEANS OF PROMOTING REPENTANCE

was stirred; and he took it up, just to pass away an idle hour, and it was the means of his conversion! That promising and pious young man, the late Henry Kirke White, who had spent some years in infidelity, was brought to Christ by reading *"Scott's Force of Truth."* I could, without much difficulty, mention other instances. How many will have reason forever to bless God for such books as *"Owen on Indwelling Sin," "Allien's Alarm,"* and *"Baxter's Call to the Unconverted?"* The last mentioned book was once the instrument of converting six brothers!

THE PREACHING OF THE GOSPEL

When the apostles went forth to preach the glad tidings of pardon and peace to guilty men, what multitudes became obedient to the faith! It might well be said, in the words of the prophet, *Who are these that fly as a cloud – as doves to their windows?* In every age, the ministry of the word has been made the means of turning men from the errors and evils of the world, to the service of the true God. Though the light-minded and self-conceited have treated it with contempt, the Lord of heaven and earth has crowned it with a blessing.

> *It pleased God by the foolishness of preaching to save them that believe. (1 Corinthians 1:21).*

God has devised a way to bring banished sinners back to himself. He has settled a covenant of peace, through the atoning blood of Christ; according to which he can be just and the justifier of every one that believeth in Jesus. This he has written in his word, sealed by his Spirit, and sent by his ministers. It is not the business of a preacher to entertain men with novelties, or sooth them with flatteries; but to show them the way of salvation. Ministers are compared to watchmen. Ezekiel 3:17. It is the duty of a watchman to sound an alarm in time of danger. In this office, diligence and faithfulness are necessary. Suppose a fire should break out in a city, and the watchman were to say, "Let us hope it will soon go out again, or not spread far; it is a pity to disturb the people!" and thus suffer the flames to consume both the houses and inhabitants; would they not be guilty of the blood of such as perished by their negligence? Every faithful minister is bound to *lift up his voice as a trumpet, and tell the people of their sins and transgressions; whether they will hear, or whether they will forbear.* He is bound to give them warning, and cry in their ears, that the fire of wrath is kindled and gathering around them. Knowing the terrors of the Lord, he labors to persuade men to escape for their life, lest they be consumed.

Ministers are ambassadors; and their work is to declare the whole counsel of God, to display the unsearchable riches of Christ, and to explain the great and precious promises. With a thousand powerful arguments, and affectionate entreaties, they address themselves to the understanding and heart.

> *Now then we are ambassadors for Christ, as though God did beseech you by us: we pray you in Christ's stead, be ye reconciled to God. For he hath made him to be sin for us, who knew no sin; that we might be made the righteousness of God in him.* (2 Corinthians 5:20 and 21).

The most diligent and zealous ministers may sometimes be discouraged, and cry out,

> *Who hath believed our report, and to whom hath the arm of the Lord been revealed?* (Isaiah 53:1, John 12:38, Roman 10:16)

Yet, notwithstanding this, preaching has been in every age the great instrument in the hand of God for the conversion of precious souls. If the servants of Christ, for a long while, seem to labor in vain, as Peter and his companions in fishing toiled all night and caught nothing; when, at his command, they put down the net on the right

CHAPTER 4: ON THE MEANS OF PROMOTING REPENTANCE

side of the ship, they are filled with amazement and joy at the draught. The apostles at first preached repentance with very little success; but when the Spirit was poured out on the day of Pentecost, Peter's sermon was so effectual, that *three thousand were at once pricked in their hearts, and cried, Men and brethren, what shall we do?* At the Reformation, when Luther in Germany, Latimer in England, and Knox in Scotland, began plainly and powerfully to preach the gospel, what numbers were turned from darkness to light, and from Satan to God? And in later times, how many were brought to repentance by the zealous labors of Elliot, Brainerd, Whitefield, and others? Mr. Berridge had above a thousand persons who applied to him under serious impressions in one year, most of them awakened by his own preaching. God has sent us the treasure of the gospel truth, not that it should be shut up and concealed like the miser's gold, but freely communicated to enrich every land, and bless every believer.

> *But we have this treasure in earthen vessels, that the excellency of the power may be of God, and not of us. (2 Corinthians 4:7).*

THE USE OF PRUDENT COUNSELS, AND FAITHFUL, AFFECTIONATE REPROOFS

It is certainly the work of God to bring a wandering guilty soul to himself, but he employs various instruments for this end. *Reproofs of instruction,* says Solomon, *are the way of life.* Some have sat unmoved for years, under the most searching and powerful discourses in public, who have been effectually wrought upon by a few words of kind counsel in private. Many a strong castle that could not be forced by a whole battery of cannon, has been approached in some secret, unobserved way, and suddenly taken by surprise. In free, familiar conversation, we can drop a word of warning or advice, at the fittest time, and in the most favorable circumstances.

We can put forth a parable like Nathan, and when the way is prepared, bring home the faithful application, *Thou art the man*. The words of the wise are as nails and as goads, fastened by the masters of assemblies. It requires both skill and care so to urge these goads, so to drive and rivet these nails that they may rouse, but not provoke, and leave a lasting impression. Private Christians may in this way become useful to their relations and friends, and even to strangers.

> *Let him know, that he which converteth the sinner from the error of his way shall save a soul from death, and shall hide a multitude of sins. (James 5:20).*

Sometimes reproofs and admonitions, whether given by ministers, or others, are attended with circumstances so remarkable, that the hand of God may be seen, and the voice of God heard, to make them effectual. Mr. Thoroughgood, a minister in the days of Charles II, once so pointedly reproved swearing, that a man who thought himself particularly intended, hid himself behind a hedge, in the way which Mr. Thoroughgood usually took in going to preach his evening lecture. When he came up to the place, the man, who intended to shoot him, levelled his gun and attempted to fire, but it only flashed in the pan. The next week he went to the same place to renew his attack, but the very same event happened. The man's conscience immediately smote him; he went to Mr. Thoroughgood, fell on his knees, and with tears in his eyes related his design to him, and asked for his forgiveness. This providence was the means of his conversion.

AFFLICTION

God often makes the plowshare of calamity break up the stubborn soil, before he showers down his softening influences. The most painful events are sometimes blessed, to bring men to a sense of their sin and danger. Of all the kings that reigned over Judah, there was none so

CHAPTER 4: ON THE MEANS OF PROMOTING REPENTANCE

wicked as Manasseh; he was not only guilty of the most gross profaneness and vile adultery, but he also made the streets of Jerusalem to run with blood, and cruelly sacrificed his children to Moloch. When he was taken captive among the thorns, he was pierced to the heart, cried to God, humbled himself greatly, and obtained pardon. 2 Chronicles 33:11 and 12. He had been a daring sinner, and now became a deep mourner. The most severe affliction, which brings a lost, wandering sinner to God, may be truly called a messenger of mercy. How many have had reason to bless God, for the most painful, bereaving providences, or the most dangerous and tedious diseases. Oh! says one, if I had been hurried into eternity before the death of such a dear friend, or such a near relation, what would have been my condition? But that which I thought my greatest loss, has through sanctifying grace, proved my greatest gain! And, Oh! says another, if I had been cut off before such a severe illness seized my body, what would have become of my soul? It was in that deep affliction, that God visited me, and brought sin to remembrance! It was then, that conscience awoke from its slumber, and began to pierce me with a thousand stings! How vain, empty, and unsatisfying did the world appear! How distressing was the review of the past! How gloomy the prospect of the future! It was then, I began to forget the pain of the body, in the keener anguish of a wounded spirit! Then I earnestly cried to the great Physician, for the healing balm of Gilead. Nor was my worthless prayer despised. Blessed be the name of Jesus! he had compassion on me, and stretched out his hand to save. He opened my ears, touched my heart, and sealed instruction to me! Ruined and undone, without help, and almost beyond hope, he passed by me, and my time of grief was his time of love!

I shall now endeavor to make it appear, that it is our duty properly to use the means for producing repentance.

REPENTANCE EXPLAINED AND ENFORCED

ANSWERING NOTIONS AGAINST THE MEANS USED FOR PRODUCING REPENTANCE

Some entertain the notion, that it is wrong to exhort sinners to repent, or use any means for that end. On what is this notion grounded? For the most part, on some wild and inconsistent idea of God's decrees. It is useless, say such people, to preach repentance; for if we are to be saved, we shall be saved, and if we are to be lost, we shall be lost. This notion is contrary to scripture, to experience, and to common sense; and agreeable to nothing but the love of sin, the will of Satan.

The Notion I oppose is Contrary to Scripture

John the Baptist, who was full of the Holy Ghost, exhorted the worst of men, even those whom he called a generation of vipers, to repent and bring forth fruits meet for repentance. Matthew 3:2, 7 and 8. Christ began his ministry, by saying,

Repent ye, and believe the gospel. (Mark 1:15).

The apostles, all of them, addressed themselves to carnal and wicked men, earnestly and constantly calling them to repentance. Paul tells us, that he testified both to the Jews and also to the Greeks, repentance towards God, and faith towards our Lord Jesus Christ. Acts 20:21. Peter perceived that Simon Magus had neither part nor lot in the matter, but was in the gall of bitterness, and the bond of iniquity. Did he turn away, and refuse to warn and exhort him? No, he said to him,

Repent therefore of this thy wickedness, and pray God, if perhaps the thought of thine heart may be forgiven thee. (Acts 8:22 and 23).

James says,

Draw nigh to God, and he will draw nigh to you. Cleanse your hands, ye sinners; and purify your hearts, ye double minded. Be afflicted, and mourn,

CHAPTER 4: ON THE MEANS OF PROMOTING REPENTANCE

and weep: let your laughter be turned to mourning, and your joy to heaviness. Humble yourselves in the sight of the Lord, and he shall lift you up. (James 4:8-10).

If it be wrong to exhort sinners to repentance, then John the Baptist, Jesus Christ, and all the apostles were in error.

The Notion I oppose is Contrary to Experience

Who are the men that have turned many to righteousness? Who are the ministers that most frequently behold vile blasphemers, under their preaching, with streaming eyes, and uplifted hands exclaim, Lord, save, or we perish? Are they those who love to dispute and wrangle, and seem to feel a savage pleasure in thundering out the harshest censures against all who differ from them? No; it cannot be denied, that those men have had most success in the conversion of souls, who have made frequent and faithful appeals to the consciences of the ungodly, in the most searching language, and solemn manner. Those whose bowels have yearned with compassion over their perishing fellow-men; whose hearts have glowed with zeal to bring them to Christ; have seen the hand of God working with them. "Some people," said the excellent Philip Henry, "do not like to hear much of repentance, but I think it so necessary, that if I should die in the pulpit, I wish to die preaching repentance, and if out of the pulpit, practicing it."

The Notion I here oppose is Contrary to Common Sense

If we are to be saved, we shall be saved, and if we are to repent, we must repent, whether we use means or not, for God has fore-ordained whatsoever comes to pass. Now suppose a man were to talk in this way concerning temporal or worldly matters. He is a husbandman, and says, I will not cultivate my land, for if I have a crop I shall have it, whether I plow and sow or not. He is sick, and a

REPENTANCE EXPLAINED AND ENFORCED

remedy is recommended which has cured many of the same disorder; but he says, no, my time is fixed, and if I am to die, all the medicines in the world cannot save me, and therefore I will use no means. Were anyone to talk thus, would it not betray a want of common sense? What can be more foolish and absurd, than to set up the secret decrees of God against his plain and well known commands! If any of the poor creatures who are chained in Bedlam, were to utter such things in their wild ravings, nobody would wonder at it. But you may say, how could such a strange notion as this enter into man's head? Or if it should spring up in a midnight dream, how can one who is awake cherish it for a moment? I reply, the notion which opposes the use of means to promote repentance, is very agreeable to the love of sin. He who delights in his own abominations, will generally hunt about for something to excuse them. Truth is against him, and he therefore sets himself against the truth. He welcomes that doctrine, be it what it may, which gives his conscience a little present ease. Now what can be more agreeable to such a person, than to hear that means are unnecessary and useless? If he wants to go on in a bold career of wickedness, he cannot have a better spur. If he wishes to sleep undisturbed, he cannot find a softer pillow.

The Notion which opposes the Use of Means to Promote Repentance, is Agreeable to the Will of the Devil

If Satan were permitted to take a human form, and become a preacher, I have no doubt he would very zealously spread this pestilent error. He would labor to keep men from all the means of grace, that he might firmly hold them as his captives. Instead of preaching repentance, he would preach presumption, and quote the scriptures too, studiously misapplying them, to carry his point. When he tempted Christ to cast himself down from a pinnacle of the temple, he backed his hellish suggestion with a text, saying,

CHAPTER 4: ON THE MEANS OF PROMOTING REPENTANCE

"For it is written, He shall give his angels charge concerning thee: and in their hands they shall bear thee up, lest at any time thou dash thy foot against a stone." (Matthew 4:6).

As though he had said, God has decreed and promised thee safety, and there can therefore be no danger or hurt from the fall. And I am sorry to have reason to say it, but there are some Antinomians of the present day, who could not have had much worse principles, if they had received their creed ready made from the devil.

Let me hope, reader, you are convinced, that

REPENTANCE IS A DUTY, AS WELL AS A PRIVILEGE

You are called to the proper use of means for this end. Do you ask, how these means are to be used? I answer – with serious consideration and prayer.

The Bible is put in your hands.

Christ expressly commands us to search the scriptures. John 5:39. Do not just carelessly look into them, and then lay them aside. Let it be your aim to learn what is *that good, and acceptable, and perfect, will of God* revealed in them. Some will not read the Bible, lest it should make them uneasy, and fill them with gloomy thoughts. Does not this prove, that they need what they neglect? Let me earnestly entreat you, to apply to the scriptures with a sincere desire to know yourself, and to know Christ, who is *the way, the truth, and the life*. Weigh your state in this balance of truth; and, when you find yourself wanting, weep over your deficiency. Lay your bosom open to this sword of the Spirit; and when you find yourself wounded, seek the healing balm of divine grace. And, besides serious consideration, lift up your heart to God, for the unction of his Holy Spirit to teach you. Let your cry be Lord, *Open thou mine eyes, that I may behold*

REPENTANCE EXPLAINED AND ENFORCED

wondrous things out of thy law. Show me thy way, and all my wanderings from it. Show me thy glory, that I may be deeply sensible of my sin, and filled with grief and shame. *Who can understand his errors? Cleanse thou me from secret faults.*

You have an opportunity of hearing the gospel.

Keep thy foot when thou goest to the house of God, and be more ready to hear, than to give the sacrifice of fools: for they consider not that they do evil. (Ecclesiastes 5:1).

The preaching of the gospel was not intended for your amusement, but for your profit. Think, when you walk to the house of God, for what purpose are you going? Think, how many Sabbaths and sermons have been lost! While you are entering the doors of the church, or chapel, carry along with you the caution our Lord has given: *Take heed how you hear!* Do the cares of this world follow you? drive them away, as Abraham drove away the birds which came down to devour his sacrifice. Do vain thoughts rush into the mind? cast them out, and give them no place or indulgence. Pray for divine grace, to render the Word quick and powerful to you. Let your heart be poured out into such petitions as these, "O Lord! thou hast sent thy gospel to my ears – apply it to my heart! Thou hast cast my lot where the light shines around me; O, let it shine into my mind, and give me glorious discoveries of thy great salvation! Gracious God! let the next sermon I hear dissolve my soul. Let the bonds of iniquity be broken, and the lusts of the flesh subdued. May I not only hear, but also understand, inwardly digest, remember, and practice thy Word!" Reading and hearing are means so valuable, that nothing can make up for the want of them. The rich man, in Luke chapter sixteen, wished Lazarus to be sent to warn his ungodly relations, and said, "If one rise from the dead they will repent; but Abraham answered, They have Moses and

CHAPTER 4: ON THE MEANS OF PROMOTING REPENTANCE

the prophet; if they hear not them, neither will they be persuaded, though one rose from the dead."

Perhaps you hear some counsels and reproofs in private. If it be so, do not make light of them. He is your best friend, who labors to awaken you to a sight of your danger, while a refuge is open to receive you. Let not pride and anger lead you to return evil for good.

> *He, that being often reproved hardeneth his neck, shall suddenly be destroyed, and that without remedy. (Proverbs 29:1).*

You have, no doubt, been visited with affliction, in one form or another; and how have you acted under it? Alas! how many are seared, rather than softened by fiery trials! God inflicts stroke upon stroke, and sends blast after blast; but instead of humbling themselves, they rise to greater heights of insolence and presumption. Such are the men spoken of by the prophets.

> *O, LORD, are not thine eyes upon the truth? thou hast stricken them, but they have not grieved; thou hast consumed them, but they have refused to receive correction: they have made their faces harder than a rock; they have refused to return. (Jeremiah 5:3).*

Do these words apply justly to you? The Lord has smitten you with the rod, but you do not repent of your folly. God has cast you into the furnace of affliction, and yet you are not melted; God has often put you under the hammer of his word, and yet you are not broken! In the time of affliction, call in your wandering thoughts and raise them to God. This is the counsel of the wise man, *In the day of prosperity, be joyful; but in the day of adversity, consider.* Pour out your fervent desires and supplications to God. *I have surely heard Ephraim bemoaning himself thus;*

REPENTANCE EXPLAINED AND ENFORCED

Thou hast chastised me, and I was chastised, as a bullock unaccustomed to the yoke: turn thou me, and I shall be turned; for thou art the LORD my God. Surely after that I was turned, I repented; and after that I was instructed, I smote upon my thigh: I was ashamed, yea, even confounded, because I did bear the reproach of my youth. (Jeremiah 31:18 and 19).

This is the temper in which affliction ought to leave us, or it is useless.

I will subjoin a few particular directions,

IN ORDER TO PROMOTE REPENTANCE

Meditate on the Shortness of Time, and the Awful Importance of Eternity

For this purpose, retire from the busy crowd. While you are pressed on all sides by the throng, and at once stunned with the noise, and blinded by the dust of the world, you can no more think calmly, than a man can walk steadily in a hurricane. The more you are engaged with the giddy multitude, the more you are likely to be infected with their spirit. O, retire into solitude that you may look beyond the narrow bounds of time, to an eternal world! Some have thought, that if even an atheist were two or three shut up in a dungeon, he would not come out an atheist. However this be, it is found by experience, that solitary tends much to dispose the mind to the great concerns of a future state. Try, then, to shake off, for a time, the cares of the world. *Commune with your own heart upon your bed, and be still.* Who knows but the hour of your departure is at hand? Do not rest contented with vague, general notions of another world; or with a few loose, shapeless wishes for future happiness. When you are about to enter on a new business, you think it needful to make some preparation. When you have a journey to take, you get things in readiness. And is there no preparation for an everlasting state? It is possible, the death-warrant may be signed, and the dreadful

CHAPTER 4: ON THE MEANS OF PROMOTING REPENTANCE

summons to appear before God is on its way. At most, in a few more years, you must go the way whence you shall not return. And dare you give up the scanty pittance of your time to levity and forgetfulness? Do you think your will is sufficient to justify your way? Have you no regard to consequences? Know certainly, "that will *without* reason, is but a blind man's motion; and will *against* reason, is but a mad man's motion." Your sins do not now trouble you, because they are not seen. And why are they not seen? The writing on a tablet, while covered with dust, cannot be discerned; but wipe it clean, and every eye can read it. "As time (says Matthew Henry) cannot wear out guilt, neither can it blot out the records of conscience." How many sins, which you now have forgotten, will rise up in remembrance on a dying bed! *O that you were wise; that you understood this; that you would consider your latter end*! Popilus, the Roman ambassador, when he went to make a very important proposal to Antiochus, king of Syria, drew a circle round him, and declared he should not pass over it, till he had given an answer. You have offended the God of heaven! He has sent his ambassadors to propose terms of peace; you are enclosed with the narrow circle of time; and you must not pass over it until this matter is settled one way or another. *Yet a little while, and he that shall come, will come, and will not tarry*. If you are not reconciled now, you will be rejected in the great day. O, may you, with sincere prayer, draw nigh to God, saying, *Lord, so teach me to number my days that I may apply my heart to wisdom*.

Meditate on the Glorious Perfections of God

How strikingly is human folly discovered by the clear display of infinite wisdom! How contemptible does pride look, while we eye the majesty of the Most High! How odious does all sin appear, in the full view of divine justice and sovereign, super-abounding grace! Jeshurun, in prosperity, *forsook God which made him, and lightly*

REPENTANCE EXPLAINED AND ENFORCED

esteemed the Rock of his salvation. (Deuteronomy 32:15). Ignorance, or forgetfulness of God, always draws after it ingratitude and disobedience. I have heard of a person, who constantly carried the picture of his father with him, and, when he was tempted to any thing wrong or dangerous, used to look at it, that the memory of his father's virtue might preserve him from vice. If the picture of a father, who was dead, increased the abhorrence of what was evil, how much more ought the presence of our heavenly Father, who searches the secrets of the heart, excite and keep up our hatred of sin! The angels above, full of reverence and love, perpetually cry, "Holy, holy, holy, is the LORD of hosts!" If you have right views of God, you will have just thoughts of yourself. The nearer you draw to a Being of infinite purity and perfection, the clearer will be the discoveries of your own depravity and defilement, worthlessness and meanness.

> "How then can man be justified with God? or how can he be clean that is born of a woman? Behold even to the moon, and it shineth not; yea, the stars are not pure in his sight. How much less man, that is a worm? and the son of man, which is a worm?" (Job 25:4-6.)

Hear Moses exclaim,

> Who is like unto thee, O LORD, among the gods? who is like thee, glorious in holiness, fearful in praises, doing wonders?" (Exodus 15:11).

Job says,

> I have heard of thee by the hearing of the ear: but now mine eye seeth thee. Wherefore I abhor myself, and repent in dust and ashes. (Job 42:5 and 6).

When Isaiah had so bright a vision of God's glory, how did it abase him in his own mind!

> Then said I, Woe is me! for I am undone; because I am a man of unclean lips, and I dwell in the midst of

CHAPTER 4: ON THE MEANS OF PROMOTING REPENTANCE

> *a people of unclean lips: for mine eyes have seen the King, the LORD of hosts.* (Isaiah 6:5).

Meditate on the Life, the Amazing Love, and the Sin-Atoning Death of Jesus Christ

Are you stupefied through the power of sin? Open the New Testament, and there behold Emmanuel. What words of wisdom and instruction flowed from his lips! What works and wonders have been done by his hands! He came not to call the righteous, but sinners to repentance. All the warnings he spake, and all the wonders he wrought, were for this end. He was grieved when he saw the hardness of their hearts, and he wept over those who never shed a tear themselves. One of the first miracles, says Henry, which Moses wrought, was turning water into blood; but one of the first miracles our Lord wrought, was turning water into wine. For the law was given by Moses, and it was a dispensation of death and terror; but grace and truth, which, like wine, make glad the heart, came by Jesus Christ. As you have greater privileges than the heathen, if you die unconverted, you must endure greater punishments; you will be accounted more guilty than the hardened and obstinate Pharaoh. Even reason itself leads us to this conclusion. But when we look into the scriptures, it is placed beyond a doubt. Better were it that you were born and brought up among barbarians, than to have the light of the gospel, and die stupefied in your sins.

> *Then began he to upbraid the cities wherein most of his mighty works were done, because they repented not: Woe unto thee, Chorazin! woe unto thee, Bethsaida! for if the mighty works, which were done in you, had been done in Tyre and Sidon, they would have repented long ago in sackcloth and ashes. But I say unto you, It shall be more tolerable for Tyre and Sidon at the day of judgment, than for you.* (Matthew 11:20-22).

REPENTANCE EXPLAINED AND ENFORCED

Meditate Seriously and Daily on the Wonderful Love of Christ

What else so well deserves to engage your thoughts? The kindness and love of God our Savior towards men, furnish a mystery, into which angels desire to look. They came down from heaven to sing a song of praise at the birth of Jesus. And while angels are filled with wonder and joy in considering the glorious scheme of human redemption, have you no thoughts to employ upon it? O turn aside, and see this great sight, the Son of God clothed in flesh to snatch us from destruction. He loved us when we had nothing to render us worthy of his love. While we were sunk in sin and misery, he left the shining regions of glory to raise us, to be partakers of his kingdom. Set, then, Christ, in all his perfection and condescension, before you. Meditate deeply, and meditate daily on him;

> that ye, being rooted and grounded in love, May be able to comprehend with all saints what is the breadth, and length, and depth, and height; And to know the love of Christ, which passeth knowledge. (Ephesians 3:17-19).

And O, how wonderful was the manner, in which Jesus manifested his love to men. He gave himself an offering and a sacrifice for us. It was absolutely impossible to have a stronger proof of love to a lost world. The apostle speaks of it as a matter of doubt, or a mere peradventure, whether any one could be found, who would dare to die, even for a good man. But while we were yet sinners and enemies, Christ died for us. Romans 5:7 and 8. He submitted to bear the curse, that we might be set free, and enjoy the blessing, even life for evermore. What can so effectually touch all the springs of sympathy in the heart as the love of Christ? And where can the love of Christ be so fully seen, as on the hill of Calvary? Draw nigh, then, to the cross; and behold the Lamb of God taking away the sin of the world. The sun withdrew his beams, the solid rocks

CHAPTER 4: ON THE MEANS OF PROMOTING REPENTANCE

rent, and the earth quaked, while Jesus suffered the penalty of our transgressions. And can you, unmoved, contemplate the awful scene? While you stand at the foot of the cross, you may sing of mercy and of judgment. While you view a suffering Savior, you may well shed tears of grief and of joy. Here are at once displayed, the terrors of injured justice, and the wonders of infinite love. Are you in any measure concerned about your eternal welfare? Turn not to Mount Sinai. There you may see your sin, but no sin-atoning sacrifice. There you may hear your doom, but no cheering voice of mercy. The law terrifies and distracts, but the law-fulfilling Surety melts and renews the soul. It is the influence of the Holy Spirit, that produces that penitence which is the beginning of a holy life. Now this is done, by turning the eye of the mind to fix on the dying Redeemer.

> *And I will pour upon the house of David, and upon the inhabitants of Jerusalem, the spirit of grace and of supplications: and they shall look upon me whom they have pierced, and they shall mourn for him, as one mourneth for his only son, and shall be in bitterness for him, as one that is in bitterness for his firstborn. (Zechariah 12:10).*

If you look to Jesus, and he look on you, the stone within your breast will be dissolved. The cock's shrill crowing stirred up Peter's memory, but so deeply was he stupefied, that a clap of thunder would not have alarmed his conscience. Yet when Jesus looked upon him, he was penetrated to the heart, and went out and wept bitterly.

CHAPTER 5
ON THE EVIDENCES OF REPENTANCE

While some persons sink under groundless fears, others are buoyed up with false and flattering hopes. The sincere but weak believer is apt to think the work of conversion is yet to begin, while the self-righteous concluded it is already done. Both are deceived, but the deception is far from being in both cases equally dangerous. Ungrounded fear may rob you of present comfort, but blind presumption will ruin you forever. It is possible, by carefully applying the scriptures to ourselves, to know whether we have been brought to repentance or not. And if this be possible, it is certainly desirable. I shall first show what are no evidences of true repentance, and next what are.

I shall show,

WHAT ARE NO EVIDENCES OR PROOFS OF TRUE REPENTANCE

To turn from one party to another is no proof of repentance. There has always been an endless variety of religious opinions and ceremonies in the world. Christians themselves are split into a great many parties and denominations. A man may often change his opinions, and never be himself changed by the gospel. He may be converted from one party to another, and never be converted to God. There are numbers who seem to be deceived by such changes.

> For he is not a Jew, which is one outwardly; neither is that circumcision, which is outward in the flesh: But he is a Jew, which is one inwardly; and circumcision is that of the heart, in the spirit, and not in the letter; whose praise is not of men, but of God. (Romans 2:28 and 29).

CHAPTER 5: ON THE EVIDENCES OF REPENTANCE

With equal truth we may say, he is not a Christian who is so in name, in form, and in profession only. If baptism made true Christians, you would, as Allein says, have only to search the parish register to know whether your names are written in heaven.

A Great Deal of Labor to Keep up Fair Appearances

is no proof of true repentance.

You may have a tree in your garden tall and stately, full of leaves, and beautiful to the eye, but destitute of fruit, like the barren fig-tree which our Lord cursed. Counterfeits may have the same stamp as sterling coin, and surpass its brightness, but when brought to the touchstone and the balance, they want purity and weight. Where there is no vital godliness, we often see a studious attempt to imitate it. When the gospel was first preached, many of the converts gave the most satisfactory proof of their sincerity and zeal. They generously gave up their property to relieve the poor, and assist in spreading the truth. Ananias and Sapphira, that they might not seem behind the rest, sold a possession, and by an agreement between themselves, kept back part of the price, and took the other part and laid it at the apostles' feet. Acts 5: 1 and 2. Though at bottom they were covetous, yet they wished to be thought liberal, and therefore contrived a low trick to gain their end. How awfully were they struck dead by the just vengeance of God for their hypocrisy!

No persons were more exact than the Pharisees, in paying tithe of mint, annis, and cumin: but it was done to conceal the neglect of the weightier matters of judgment, mercy, and faith. How often do we find people who too nearly resemble them, and take great pains merely to keep up a fair appearance! They would not for the world neglect going their round of duties, but are total strangers to the religion of the heart. It is a much easier thing to whitewash a house on the outside, than to take away the rotten beams and mouldered bricks, and rebuild it with solid materials. A man may have the garb of a penitent, and the speech of a believer, and not have one drop of sincere sorrow, or one grain of precious faith in his heart. If Noah, instead of pitching the ark to keep out the water, had only painted it to make a fair show, he would have perished like others, by the flood. Let him that thinketh he standeth take heed lest he fall.

Sudden Terrors, or Melancholy Thoughts

are no proofs of true repentance.

On the near approach of danger, or under affliction, the most presumptuous wretches have cried out for fear, as if they had been seized by ghastly fiends. It is said, Caligula, the Roman emperor, who was one of the bloodiest tyrants, though in general, he impiously defied both earth and heaven, always began to tremble and pray when it thundered and lightened. While terrible plagues were upon Pharaoh, when the magicians, with all their enchantments, could not quiet his fears, he often sent for Moses and Aaron in hast, entreated their prayers, and promised to let them go; but no sooner had he obtained deliverance, then he became harder than before. How often, when wicked men are laid on a bed of sickness, and think death very near, do they send for ministers to pray with them, and seemed much affected and alarmed at the prospect of eternity. In a little while they recover, and all their concern about religion is gone. They resemble sailors who pray in a tempest, when they are expecting the next billow to bury them in the sea; but all their devotion ceases when the storm is over, and they return again to their drinking and swearing, with redoubled eagerness. When the unclean spirit is cast out by divine grace, he cannot regain possession; but when he goes out of his own accord, he is sure to return to his old house and his old haunts, and the last end of that man is worse than the first.

CHAPTER 5: ON THE EVIDENCES OF REPENTANCE

Some persons are frequently filled with gloomy and melancholy thoughts. At such times they leave their gay companions, and sigh and weep alone. But this kind of sorrow may rise from worldly losses and disappointments, or from weakness and disorder of body, rather than from any serious concern about God, or the salvation of the soul. Sometimes we see melancholy thoughts, and terrors of conscience in the same person. Alas, how many in this unhappy state have rashly seized the murderous knife, and cut the thread of life with their own hands. King Saul was once among the prophets, and often among the gloomy penitents; he went for counsel to the witch of Endor, and after trying many bad ways to get rid of his burden, he chose the worst at last, and fell upon his own sword. The wretched Judas repented that he had betrayed innocent blood, and then went and hanged himself, that he might go to his *own* place. While he held the office of an apostle, he was quite out of his own place. What right has the wolf in the sheepfold, or a devil to take his seat among the disciples of Jesus? But Satan, when occasion requires, can put on Samuel's mantle, or even transform himself into an angel of light.

Lively Joys, and Confident Hopes

are no proofs of true repentance.

There is something peculiarly grand and important in the doctrines of the gospel. Now, it sometimes happens, that those who are brought under the sound of the gospel, are at first struck with admiration. They profess that their views and sentiments are changed, and that they are become new creatures. They tell us in strong language how wonderfully they are delighted with gospel promises, and seem as sure of heaven as those who dwell there. Yet all this is merely a flash in the imagination; not a steady light in the understanding, or a flame of holy love in the heart. It is the dream of fancy, not the joy of faith. Such were the stony-ground hearers mentioned by our Lord. Matthew

REPENTANCE EXPLAINED AND ENFORCED

13:20 and 21. They quickly received the word with joy, but having no root soon withered away.

Herod heard John the Baptist gladly, and did many things which were commendable. He could not, however, bear to be reproved for the sake of Herodias. He soon proved, that though he had been pleased with the preacher, he had not been profited by his doctrine. When his birthday came, instead of beginning a new year of his life with penitence for the past, and prayer for the future, he began it with mirth and murder. He ordered the Baptist's head to be cut off, to gratify and infamous woman.

If you have lively joys and confident hopes, examine whence they spring, and what is their tendency. Bring your feelings as well as your faith to the touchstone of God's Word. Many begin to rejoice before they have any just ground. When they are dealt with plainly and faithfully, they are offended. The wounds of the conscience cannot be healed without probing, nor probed without pain. If then, like Herod, you have some particular sin for which you cannot bear reproof, you are deceiving yourself by supposing your joys are a proof of your conversion.

I shall now point out,

WHAT ARE THE EVIDENCES OF REAL REPENTANCE

A true penitent will forsake his sin, renounce the world, resist the devil, love Christ, and long to be fully conformed to him.

A True Penitent will Forsake His Sin.

If a man had often reproached and wronged you, and professed to be sorry for it, could you believe him sincere unless he altered his conduct? Solomon says,

CHAPTER 5: ON THE EVIDENCES OF REPENTANCE

> *He that covereth his sins shall not prosper: but whoso confesseth and forsaketh them shall have mercy. (Proverbs 28:13).*

A thousand flimsy disguises are woven, and a thousand vain excuses contrived, to conceal sin. To hide the accursed thing, Achan took his Babylonish garment and his wedge of gold, and buried them in his tent. The true penitent is willing to lay aside every plea for sin, and give up the practice of it. He who hates sin for its own sake, will pray to be delivered from its power, as well as from its punishment. "There are some persons,' says an old writer, "notoriously wicked, who swallow sin down, actually and openly committing it. Others hide their sin under their tongues, spare it, and forsake it not, but keep it still within their mouths. Job 20:12. But penitents spit it out as the worst poison, loathing it in their judgment, and leaving it in their practice."

> *For godly sorrow worketh repentance to salvation not to be repented of: but the sorrow of the world worketh death. For behold this selfsame thing, that ye sorrowed after a godly sort, what carefulness it wrought in you, yea, what clearing of yourselves, yea, what indignation, yea, what fear, yea, what vehement desire, yea, what zeal, yea, what revenge! In all things ye have approved yourselves to be clear in this matter. (2 Corinthians 7:10 and 11).*

Some profess to be converted by the gospel, but if they did not tell us so, we should never know it. There is no appearance of a change in the heart, from any change of life. They remain as light-minded, as ill-tempered, as full of the world, as frothy in their conversation, and as loose in their walk as ever. Be not deceived. Bring forth fruits meet for repentance, for by such fruits only can it be known. The convictions which are not strong enough to subdue the dominion of sin, and deep enough to penetrate to the bottom of the heart, are of no real use. Has the fornicator become chaste, and the drunkard sober? Has the swearer learned to fear an oath, and the Sabbath-breaker to honor the sacred day? Has the careless become thoughtful, the proud humble, the passionate meek? Is the vulture turned into a dove, and the lion into a lamb?

Nor is it enough to forsake crimes of the blackest or grossest sort, and yet live in the practice of other sins. If you determine to indulge one lust, though in a cautious and concealed way, it will prove your destruction. As the least sin was painful to Christ, so it is hateful to God, and hurtful to the soul. A man will as certainly bleed to death of a single wound, if it be not stanched and healed, as if he were stabbed with a hundred daggers. A ship will sink as surely, though not quite so speedily, from one small leak unstopped, as from the bursting of a whole plank. Can you say, with David,

> Therefore I esteem all thy precepts concerning all things to be right; and I hate every false way. (Psalm 119:128)?

Can you part with the idols you have most loved and adored? Do you set yourself against secret sins, as much as against those which are open and well known?

If you truly hate sin, you will not fail to shun the occasions which lead to it.

The path in which you walk is full of dangers. Many things, not evil in themselves, may be occasions of evil to us. That which proves a snare to one, may be none to another. Do you know your weak side, and place a double guard there? Are you acquainted with the sin which most easily besets you? Do you make Job's covenant with your eyes, and use David's bridle for your tongue? Do you abstain from the very appearance of evil? When you are placed in a strait, do you choose to suffer rather than to sin? Excess of caution is better than self-confidence. You had better, says one, use bolts and locks, than leave the

CHAPTER 5: ON THE EVIDENCES OF REPENTANCE

least door of danger open. He who prays not to be led into temptation, and then goes forth to meet it, is like a man who begs he may not be hurt, and immediately puts his foot upon a wasp's nest, or his hand into the fire.

The same hatred to sin, which leads a penitent to shun its allurements, makes him thankful for every restraint that prevents his committing it, when he is either provoked by ill treatment, or taken by surprise. David being shamefully insulted by that foul-tongued churl, Nabal, went forth in the heat of his anger to revenge the injury he had received. How thankful was he for the counsel of Abigail, and the gracious providence which sent her to meet him.

> *And David said to Abigail, Blessed be the LORD God of Israel, which sent thee this day to meet me: And blessed be thy advice, and blessed be thou, which hast kept me this day from coming to shed blood, and from avenging myself with mine own hand. (1 Samuel 25:32 and 33).*

And I will go a step further, and observe that, where repentance is sincere, it will not only lead a man to break off the practice of sin, but also to repair, as far as possible, the mischief he has done. If you have slandered and degraded others, you ought to confess it, and make all the satisfaction in your power. When Zacchaeus was converted, he became both generous and just. He was willing to give the half of his goods to the poor, and restore four-fold to those whom he had wronged. A servant woman, in whom her master placed great confidence, but who had robbed him at various times to a considerable amount, was awakened under the ministry of Mr. Pomfret. Some years after, Mr. Pomfret was insisting upon restitution, as a necessary part of repentance; upon which she brought the money to Mr. Pomfret, acknowledging what she had done, who immediately returned it to his son, saying, "Sir, you see the good effects of the Word of God."

REPENTANCE EXPLAINED AND ENFORCED

Do you hate sin? flee from it. Do you watch and pray against its allurements? You, perhaps, reply, "I do hate it; yet I cannot keep it under. I pluck it up, and cast it out; but, the roots remaining, it springs up afresh. O! my vain thoughts and ungoverned passions! how they grieve and trouble me!" It was said by Daniel Burgess, "The field which had millions of weeds in it, is, nevertheless, a cornfield." Though many sins rise, if you are a penitent, they do not reign. You will not allow sin, but carry on a constant war against it.

A True Penitent Renounces the World

Do you startle with surprise! Mistake not my meaning. I do not mean that you should give up your business, or have no dealing with ungodly men. This, as it would be almost impossible, would be highly improper. Nor do I mean that you should be of a sour or unsociable temper, as though it were a sin to treat others with civility and kindness. Were you to go and dwell in a wilderness, it would be no proof of a contrite heart, or a humble spirit. To renounce the world in the best sense, is, to give up its false maxims and opinions, its foolish amusements and dangerous pleasures. You must part with all these, if you would cleave with purpose of heart to the Lord. The spirit of the world, and the spirit of the gospel, are as opposite as light and darkness. Jesus said,

> *No man can serve two masters: for either he will hate the one, and love the other; or else he will hold to the one, and despise the other. Ye cannot serve God and mammon. (Matthew 6:24).*

To endeavor to unite things, which have nothing in which they can agree, is all lost labor.

> *Love not the world, neither the things that are in the world. If any man love the world, the love of the Father is not in him. (1 John 2:15).*

CHAPTER 5: ON THE EVIDENCES OF REPENTANCE

God has plainly forbidden you to follow a multitude to do evil. Bad examples have a great power to draw men into sin. From the time you become penitent and pious, you are not allowed to mix with the worldly-minded and wicked, lest they should beguile or ensnare you.

> *Wherefore come out from among them, and be ye separate, saith the Lord, and touch not the unclean thing; and I will receive you, And will be a Father unto you, and ye shall be my sons and daughters, saith the Lord Almighty. (2 Corinthians 6:17 and 18). And be not conformed to this world: but be ye transformed by the renewing of your mind, that ye may prove what is that good, and acceptable, and perfect, will of God. (Romans 12:2).*

And now let me ask you, can you despise the smiles, the flatteries, and pleasures of the world? It presents a thousand charms to entice and entrap you. "The wise man (say Bishop Hopkins) sums up the whole value of the world in a great cypher and a great blot – vanity and vexation!" Experience proves this account to be just. Do you turn away, and cry, Farewell, vain world! I have too long been mocked with thy fair shows and dancing shadows! I have too long believed thy false promises, and followed thy pernicious ways! I have too long drunk the cup of thy poisonous sweets, and worn thy gaudy livery of divers colors! Being enlightened from above, I cannot admire, and will not obey thee! And what is all thy boasted happiness? "A notion – a day dream – a wish – a sigh – a theme to be talked of – a mark to be shot at, but never hit – a picture in the head – and a pang in the heart!" My time is too precious to be bartered for thy worthless toys! my soul is too valuable to be cast away for thy best treasures and honors!

But let me ask again, can you despise the frowns, reproaches, and injuries of the world?

REPENTANCE EXPLAINED AND ENFORCED

"In time of prosperity, (said Flavel), hypocrisy lies hid in the heart, like a nest in the green bushes; but when the winter of adversity has blown away the leaves, every one may see it without searching." If you are truly penitent, it will be seen in the day of trial. If you have turned to God, expect the outcries of the world against you. Can you stand the laugh of the haughty scorner? Can you bear to have your name cast out as evil? Have you courage to be singular? Doubtless, many will think it strange that ye run not with them to the same excess of riot, speaking evil of you. Can you swim against the tide, and boldly face the storm? Can you take up the cross, and go forth to Jesus without the camp, bearing his reproach? Are you prepared to meet, without flinching from your profession, the foulest falsehoods that slander can invent, and the sharpest arrows that malice can shoot? Do you, like Moses, *choose rather to suffer affliction with the people of God, than to enjoy the pleasures of sin for a season*? Luther used to say, "The Christian's life consists in three points: in faith, in love, and in the cross." Every genuine penitent is a pilgrim on the earth. You must turn your back upon the world, and go forth with weeping and supplication; earnestly asking the way to Zion, and pressing towards it. While you were in a league of friendship with the world, you were a stranger to God; and now that you are reconciled to God, you must be contented to live a stranger in the world. Do you make it manifest that you seek a better country, better society, better employment, better treasures, and better delights than any that the present world can bestow?

A True Penitent Resists the Devil

Satan is called *the god of this world; the spirit that now worketh in the children of disobedience*. He watches and guards his slaves with the jealousy of a tyrant. Though he is always active, yet we have reason to believe he is particularly busy with the young convert. When a man becomes serious and thoughtful, and begins to seek the

CHAPTER 5: ON THE EVIDENCES OF REPENTANCE

company of the pious, to read and hear the Word with attention, and pour out tears and prayers before God, this enemy will do all he can to hinder him. Is the good seed sown? he tries to catch it up and carry it away. When any one is convinced of the guilt of sin, and the necessity of flying to Christ for safety, he labors to lull him into slumber and quietness; if this scheme fails, he hurries him into the world, that he may either work away his convictions in its busy employments, or sport them away in its fluttering amusements. Having the Holy Scriptures, we are not ignorant of his devices. We are warned *of* them, that we may be armed *against* them. Now, of these devices there are two kinds, which he employs as occasion requires: he either tempts by something that allures, or terrifies by something that alarms.

He often tries to tempt, by presenting something which allures. The apostle speaks of the wiles of the devil. Simon Magus, who, it is said, a long time bewitched the people, was but an under-workman that took his lessons from this great sorcerer. He was but a bungler in the art, compared with this more subtle and successful master. Satan has a thousand methods to deceive and destroy the souls of men. How artfully does he spread his nets and hang out his false colors! How craftily does he prepare his baits, and so present them, that the hooks are neither seen nor suspected! He beguiled Eve by the fair but forbidden fruit; and since that time he has increased his skill, by long experience and great success. Then, he had but one narrow opening, as a way of approach; but now, the fences being broken down, he has many free passages. Then, he had but one lure; now, he has myriads! He can suit every state and case. Yet, as Bishop Hopkins observes, "His most prevailing temptation is worldly wealth.

> *All these things will I give thee, if thou wilt fall down and worship me. (Matthew 4:9).*

REPENTANCE EXPLAINED AND ENFORCED

When this battery could not make a breach, he raised the siege, despairing of success."

Satan often tries to terrify, by presenting something to alarm. He changes his policy to answer his purpose. If he cannot draw, he labors to drive men from religion. When a poor sinner begins to inquire what he shall do to be saved, and turns his eyes to the only sufficient Refuge, Satan says, "you have gone too far to return; your sin is too great to be forgiven! Talk not of promises; they are not for you, but for others! Think not of making prayers and confessions; for they will be vain and useless!"

Now, when this serpent would tempt you with his wiles; when this lion would terrify you with his roars, do you yield or oppose him? Do you hold parley with him? or instantly cry out, *Get thee behind me, Satan*? James says,

Resist the devil, and he will flee from you.

I answer: you have both good armor provided, and a great Captain at hand to help you. Turn not away with dastardly cowardice. If you are a true penitent, you must have many a battle with Beelzebub. And I would ask, do you now determine to resist him steadfast in the faith? Do you distrust yourself, that you may *be strong in the Lord, and in the power of his might*? Do you *take unto you the whole armor of God, that ye may be able to withstand in the evil day, and having done all, to stand*? Are *your loins girt about with truth*? Is your heart guarded with *the breastplate of righteousness*? and your head with *the helmet of salvation*? Do you *take the sword of the Spirit* in one hand, and *the shield of faith, to quench all the fiery darts of the wicked one,* in the other? Do you not only fight, but also *pray with all prayer and supplication in the Spirit*, for timely succor and deliverance? These things prove that your repentance is of the right kind. Be not dismayed; for you shall find God's grace in assisting you above Satan's malice in assaulting you.

CHAPTER 5: ON THE EVIDENCES OF REPENTANCE

A True Penitent Loves Christ, and Longs to be Conformed to His Likeness

A carnal or worldly man wonders to hear Christians speak in such affectionate and endearing language of the adorable Redeemer, and considers it all hypocrisy and delusion! But he, whose mind is enlightened, and whose heart is renewed, cries out with one of the martyrs, "None but Christ! none but Christ!" Austin tells us, that Marcellina hung the picture of Christ, and the picture of Pythagoras together, dividing her admiration between them. And are there not too many who seem to think they can give an equal share of their affection to the Savior and to the creature? But does Emmanuel, who gave himself wholly for us, deserve no more than half the heart? What! can you view the glory of God in the face of Jesus Christ, and not adore him? Can you consider his amazing condescension and kindness, and not love him? Can you think of his honorable titles and important offices, and not trust him? No! If you discern the greatness of his power, the brightness of his glory, the fullness of his grace, and the riches of his kingdom, you will cheerfully give him the throne of your heart, and account every thing else but dross and dung, compared with his excellency. Plutarch the historian relates, that when a certain lady showed her fine furniture to the wife of Phocion, and then asked what she had to show? her answer was, "My excellent husband!" When precious stones and valuable jewels were brought forth, and the same question put, she gave a similar answer: "All my wealth, honor, and happiness is in my excellent husband." Thus, a sincere Christian can say, Christ is all and in all. He is the pearl of great price – the portion of my soul! Having him, I cannot be poor; without him, the whole world could not make me rich!

> *For the love of Christ constraineth us; because we thus judge, that if one died for all, then were all dead: And that he died for all, that they which live should*

REPENTANCE EXPLAINED AND ENFORCED

not henceforth live unto themselves, but unto him which died for them, and rose again. (2 Corinthians 5:14 and 15).

What the apostle here speaks of, is not a painful, but a pleasant constraint. What band can so sweetly draw the soul, as the love of Christ! What fire can so effectually melt the heart, as the love of Christ! If you are abased for sin, it will appear in your readiness to exalt and imitate the Savior. Sometimes the sincere Christian is depressed under a consciousness of imperfection, and begins to cry out, "Alas! how small is my love to Christ! I have reason to doubt, whether I have any at all!" That you may not be discouraged, remember that it is said of Jesus,

A bruised reed shall he not break, and the smoking flax shall he not quench. (Isaiah 42:3).

He will not despise *the day of small things*. It has been justly said by an ingenious author, "One rose upon a bush, though but a little one, and not yet blown, proves that which bears it to be a true rose-tree."

There is a kind of legal repentance, which has in it no mixture of love to God, or love to holiness. Many, like Ahab, have put on sackcloth and ashes, who were never clothed with humility. They have had their frights and fits of trembling, and yet turned to their course again, as the horse rusheth into battle. Though you should repent a thousand times in this way, you would be no better for it.

Let me ask, do you own the authority of Christ as the King of Zion? and draw nigh to touch the sceptre of mercy, that you may live? Do you wish to embrace him in the arms of faith, as the only Savior? Do you see his all-sufficiency, and make an entire surrender of your soul into his hands? Can you give up every self-righteous trust, and say, Lord! I am a rebel! let me be reconciled and received with thy friends; I am a stranger – adopt me into thy family, and put me among thy children; I desire to be

CHAPTER 5: ON THE EVIDENCES OF REPENTANCE

guided by thy Word, washed in thy blood, clothed in thy righteousness, fortified by thy power, cheered with thy smiles, supplied from thy stores, and at last numbered among thy jewels?

Paul expressly affirms, that *if any man have not the Spirit of Christ, he is none of his. (Romans 8:9)*. It is impossible, truly to love Christ, and not bear something of his likeness. Every real penitent is made yielding and submissive. He is like clay; first softened, that it may be cast into the mould; and then formed into a vessel, bearing the master's name, and fitted for the master's use. Many who would be reckoned among Christians, show a lamentable deficiency in this respect: their tempers and dispositions have none of that mildness or sweetness, which the gospel ought to produce: religion has not made them more amiable and useful, than they were without it. We read of the meekness and gentleness of Christ; but we look in vain to find them in such professors as these. Now, do you wish to bear the image of Christ? Do you willingly take his yoke and wear it? Are you bold enough to confess him before men? Do you desire to learn wisdom under his teaching? Do you admire and imitate your Master? Do you wish and pray to be kind, like him; humble, like him; penitent, like him; holy, like him? Do you daily endeavor to trace his steps, and walk as he walked; sincerely mourning over all your wanderings and backslidings? Do you set before you his fair example, and, while you copy it, lament every blot occasioned through your carelessness and inattention? When others fall away, do you feel for the state of their souls, and for the dishonor cast upon religion in the world? When corruption rises up within you, and works in pride, anger, and impatience, are you more afraid of offending God and grieving his Holy Spirit, than of drawing upon you the displeasure of men? He who knows and loves Christ, will in some degree resemble him. The threatenings may sometimes frighten a man from committing bold acts of sin; but the great and precious promises only, can make him a partaker of a divine nature. But, that this may be the case, the promises must be received with faith. Every promise has its excellency from Christ, and its efficacy by faith. None but polished bodies can reflect the images of things. It would be foolish to use a lump of black earth for a looking-glass! The mind, while encrusted with ignorance, impenitence, and unbelief, can never reflect the image of Christ. When once it is renewed and become spiritual, the glorious Redeemer is then both the object it loves, and the model it imitates. And can you say, "Blessed be God, I am sick of sin and weary of the world; but Christ is altogether lovely in my eyes: I desire to have every feature of his image stamped upon my soul; I long to have my thoughts more raised and refined, and my affections more holy and ardent; I do follow his steps, whether men praise me, and copy his example, though in a very imperfect manner; I pray to be a living epistle of Christ, known and read of all men!" These are marks of sincere repentance.

From what has been said,

I SHALL MAKE A FEW OBSERVATIONS

Observe, it is,

Highly Important that You should know Whether You are Truly Penitent or Not

The generality of men are in no degree concerned about this matter. Some imagine, though without ground, that they have repented already, and therefore conclude they are safe, at all events. It is easy to see how dangerous such a notion is; and yet how prone we are to entertain it! Most men are glad of any thing, which will save them from present pain and trouble.

Suppose a man have a deep and dangerous wound in his leg or arm; he goes to a surgeon and has it examined. The surgeon says, "Friend, I am sorry your case

CHAPTER 5: ON THE EVIDENCES OF REPENTANCE

is so bad; but, I must faithfully tell you, amputation is absolutely necessary!" The man turns pale, and cries, "Oh Sir! I hope not; you must try to cure it without such a painful operation!" He replies, "It is impossible! I tell you plainly, you must lose your limb or your life; for both cannot be preserved!" The man then goes to some ignorant pretender to skill, and opens his case to him. He looks at it, and then wonders that anyone should be so rash or cruel as to talk of amputation. "It is, indeed, (says he,) a dreadful wound; but, with a little mollifying ointment and proper care, I have no doubt it will soon be healed." We may easily judge which of the two the poor man would be most ready to believe; and the advice first given might, after all, be the best. The same reasoning will hold good in regard to the state of the soul. Our Lord speaks of *cutting off and right hand*, and *plucking out a right eye*, to denote the necessity of a total separation from every beloved sin.

A day is coming that will try every man's state and work. You can lose nothing by examining yourself impartially before the Judge appears. But should you rest on an ill-grounded assurance of your salvation, and find your mistake when there can be no opportunity of rectifying what is wrong, or repenting at the foot of the cross, your state will be desperate. When Christ comes, he will bring his fan in his hand and thoroughly purge his floor. If the devil were allowed to winnow, he would soon blow away both the chaff and the corn, as with a whirlwind; but Christ will separate them, and while he gathers the wheat into his garner, without losing one precious grain, he will burn up the chaff with unquenchable fire. You may be thankful that the fan is in safe and good hands.

Observe, it is,

Very Necessary to be Careful in Examining Yourself

or your labor will all be lost. Four things have been mentioned as evidences of repentance. I shall briefly

REPENTANCE EXPLAINED AND ENFORCED

review them, and beg you to make an application to yourself as I proceed.

PERSONALLY APPLYING THE EVIDENCES OF REPENTANCE

It has been said, the true penitent forsakes sin.

Let it, however, be remembered, that it is possible to forsake the act of some particular sin for a time, and not put off the habit. We do not say, the moment it ceases to rain, the weather is fine, when we see the tempest still thick in the wind. It is a fit and familiar comparison which Gurnall uses, "We do not say that a man forsakes his house every time he leaves home, but only when he quits it with the full purpose never to return." The same may be said with respect to our forsaking sin. Where sincere repentance takes place, there will be no allowance of iniquity.

> *He that walketh righteously, and speaketh uprightly; he that despiseth the gain of oppressions, that shaketh his hands from holding of bribes, that stoppeth his ears from hearing of blood, and shutteth his eyes from seeing evil, (Isaiah 33.15)*

proves that the root of real religion is in him.

I have said that, a true penitent renounces the world.

You may reply, I have now given up my youthful follies and vain pursuits. But you have need to be careful how you judge by this rule. A man may quit the circle of fashion, plunge into the tumults of business, and at last sink into the ease of stupor of ease and indolence, and all the while remain wedded to the world. To be carnally minded, though with a considerable variety of feelings and pursuits, is death. The fever may be followed by a palsy and the issue still be fatal. The wild worldling and the tame worldling are of the same species. The difference between the youth and age of many persons, is similar to the

CHAPTER 5: ON THE EVIDENCES OF REPENTANCE

difference there is between a gay butterfly on the wing, and a sluggish worm groveling in the dust.

I have said that a true penitent resists the devil.

You may reply, This, too, I have done. Many temptations have been laid in my way with which I have refused to comply. But what made you refuse? It might be your convenience, not your conscience. Some change their sins as they do their clothes, and so wait upon their old infernal master in a new livery.

I have said that a true penitent loves Christ, and longs to be like him.

You may say, I think highly of the Redeemer, and hope to be saved by him. And how is this manifested? If you have an earthly friend, you burn with indignation to see him ill-treated, or hear him slandered and dishonored. And can you sit unmoved while scoffers blaspheme that worthy name by which we are called? Can you witness dishonor cast upon Christ and his truth, without being grieved, and roused to take off the foul reproach? Is this thy kindness to thy best friend? A real love to Christ, and a desire to be like him, cannot be hid. You must show them in various ways. Now examine yourself by these evidences.

But what shall I say to you, if, by the foregoing pages,

(If) You are Fully Convinced that You are Yet in a State of Impenitence?

There is not a moment to be lost. O, weigh well the worth of your immortal soul. Set death and judgment before you. Christ stands with open arms ready to receive you. While the gospel sounds, hear and your soul shall live. Let not gains and cares entangle you; let not toys and trifles divert you; let not errors and vain hopes delude you. Fly, fly without delay to the Redeemer. Are you saying, Lord, I come to thee? Lo! I fall at thy feet that I may put

REPENTANCE EXPLAINED AND ENFORCED

off the iron yoke of bondage, and put on thy easy yoke of obedience. I have opened my mouth and given up myself, and I cannot, I dare not go back. Lord, I will follow thee through pains and changes, through honor and dishonor. I can gladly say amen, may it be so. Witness, ye angels, and second the solemn vow. But remember when you put your hand to the plough you must not stand still, nor so much as look back, but persevere to the end. If like Peter's, your resolution rest on your own strength, like his it will assuredly fail when the trial comes. Oh, look unto Jesus, the author and finisher of faith, that you may be strengthened with all might by his Spirit in the inner man, and so run the heavenly race as to obtain the immortal prize. Observe, that,

If You have Some Evidences of Repentance

you ought not to be always doubting and complaining.

Some sincere Christians are so much engrossed with their fears, that they gain little advantage from their hopes. Such persons resemble seamen, so intent on watching the coming storm, as to lose their sheet anchor which should secure them in a hurricane. You may cry out, O, that I had but the proofs of having undergone a thorough change, and I should be happy! Would to God I could speak with the same well-grounded confidence which many can. Do not always look on the dark side of the cloud. "A repining life," said one, "is but a lingering death." Do not always hang your harp upon the willows, or tune it to melancholy strains. "Unreasonable fears are the sins of our hearts as well as thorns in our sides: they grieve the Spirit and provoke him to withdraw his comforting influences."

If you have not so bright evidence of an inward change as some have, be not always poring upon your own state, and laboring to spell out the reality of your personal religion, by the tenure of your frames and feelings. It is

CHAPTER 5: ON THE EVIDENCES OF REPENTANCE

useless to cry, Oh! that I had assurance in the same way as Elijah, or Hezekiah, Paul, or John. Having the ordinary means of grace, it is wrong to expect miracles. If the enemy can draw you into doubts and despondencies, so as to entangle the soul, he will triumph in your distress. Let nothing keep you back from the throne of grace. If you doubt whether the work is yet begun, pray that it may be begun. If you cannot go to God *with* a broken heart, go to him *for* a broken heart. He waiteth to be gracious, and is exalted to show mercy. He never said to the seed of Jacob, Seek ye me in vain.

CHAPTER 6
ON THE ENCOURAGEMENTS GIVEN TO THE PENITENT

The Savior was sent to bind up the broken-hearted, and set at liberty them that were bound. Every word in the gospel speaks encouragement to the humble. But perhaps you may say, I have no doubt that God is gracious to hear the prayer of the penitent, but I fear this is not my character. Some persons can tell the time of their awakening, and even the means which God used for that purpose, but I cannot. They can mention the books, the sermons, or the very texts which touched their hearts, and drew forth the earnest cry, What shall we do? but though I am sensible of my lost condition, it is impossible for me to trace back my concern to any particular season, or instrumental cause. Suppose a man deeply in debt thus to tell his tale to a neighbor: I have long feared that my business and my books were in a bad state, but now I am sure it is so. I cannot say exactly when, or by what means I first began to perceive this. Sometimes I suspected it, and soon after forgot my fears; then the alarm returned afresh, as my creditors brought new demands which I could not answer. This neighbor replies; of what consequence is it for you to know when you first found out your deficiency? I am acquainted with a rich friend who will be bound for you. All you have to do is, to go without delay to this surety, and commit your affairs into his hands. Would not such advice be the best? You, too, are deeply in debt. You have no means of paying the long arrears. Now if you are fully convinced of this, I recommend to you the Lord Jesus Christ, the friend of sinners. He is ready to become your security, and answer every demand. Or suppose a man to say, I have long felt myself unwell; my health is gone; but really I cannot tell when I first perceived the symptoms of my disorder. Some persons can declare

CHAPTER 6: ENCOURAGEMENTS GIVEN TO THE PENITENT

the place where, and the manner how they were first struck with pain, or seized with sickness; but alas! it is not so with me. I should say to such an one, the question is not when you began to know your disorder; do you now know it? If so, all you have to do, is to go without delay to the best physician. Thus, whenever there is a due sense of sin, I would say, hasten to the Lord Jesus Christ. It is of little consequence whether you were awakened suddenly or gradually, your chief concern now lies in the means of obtaining relief.

While I proceed to give encouragement to the penitent, I feel somewhat at a loss, not for want of matter, but to know how to select from the abundance which offers, that which may be most suitable. We can scarcely look into the Bible, but we find something to animate the contrite and humble. I have gathered a few things, and you may go to the same rich treasury, and gather the rest for yourself. After I have said a few words, I must own with the queen of Sheba, that the half cannot be told. Are you sensible of your guilt and condemnation, your want and misery, your pollution and helplessness? then I would direct you to those promises which hold out pardon, adoption, and the sanctifying power of the Holy Spirit.

THE SCRIPTURES PROMISE *PARDON* TO THE PENITENT

Forgiveness is a blessing so suitable to fallen man, so sweet and precious to the humble soul, that it cannot be too earnestly sought, or too highly valued. The angels who sinned are confined under chains of darkness unto the judgment of the great day. The call to repentance, or the sound of salvation, was never heard in hell. In that dismal prison no gleam of hope shines, no fountain of mercy flows. The Redeemer says, *To you, O men, I call, and my voice is to the sons of men*. When God pardons our sins, he is said to *blot them out,* to *remove them as far as the east is from the west*, or to *cast them into the depths of the sea*. These expressions not only throw light upon the subject of forgiveness, but also afford peculiar encouragement to the penitent. Though his sins should be never so numerous, or never so odious, they shall not appear against him for his condemnation. Though you should owe more than ten thousand talents, the book being crossed, you shall stand completely clear. Though your sins be like a cloud, which blackens the face of heaven, burdens the air, and gathers a mighty tempest, they shall be entirely and forever removed. Isaiah 45:22. This is one of the chief blessings secured to men by the glorious covenant of grace.

> *I will be merciful to their unrighteousness, and their sins and their iniquities will I remember not more. (Hebrews 8:12).*

Hebrews 8:1-12. Dr. Owen justly observes, "That the pardon bestowed by God, is not like that narrow, difficult, halving forgiveness, that is found among men, when any such thing is found among them; but it is full, free, bottomless, boundless, absolute, such as becomes his nature and excellencies." Now if you really wish this invaluable blessing, the gospel brings it in its bosom, and offers it without money and without price. God commands and invites you to accept of pardon; he pleads with you to receive it; he points to the blood of atonement, the intercession of his Son, and the examples of those who have obtained forgiveness, to prevail with you.

God Commands You to accept Pardon

After Christ had risen from the dead, he have his apostles authority to spread the glad tidings of salvation throughout the world. They were sent *to preach repentance and remission of sins to all nations, beginning at Jerusalem. (Luke 24:47)*. Astonishing mercy! How many righteous men, how many heaven-inspired prophets had been slain in that bloody city. There, the Messiah himself was mocked and buffeted, condemned and crucified. Who would have wondered, if he had said, Go and preach

CHAPTER 6: ENCOURAGEMENTS GIVEN TO THE PENITENT

repentance and remission of sins everywhere, except in that devoted city, Jerusalem? The apostles zealously obeyed the order of their master, as appears from Acts 2:28 onward.

> *Repent ye therefore, and be converted, that your sins may be blotted out, when the times of refreshing shall come from the presence of the Lord. (Acts 3:19).*

There, it may be seen, that pardon follows penitence. What God has joined, must not, cannot be put asunder. You are as much commanded to receive forgiveness, as you are to repent. Do not then resist the authority of God through unbelief. Say not, I am so vile, that there can be no forgiveness extended to me. The blessing is held out in the promise, and the command requires you to take it.

Mr. Marshall, author of a treatise on Sanctification, in his early years was under great distress for a long time, through a consciousness of guilt and a dread of the divine displeasure. At last mentioning his ease to Dr. Thomas Goodwin, and lamenting the greatness of his sins, that able divine replied, "You have forgotten the greatest sin of all, the sin of unbelief in refusing to believe in Christ, and rely on his atonement and righteousness for your acceptance with God." This word in season banished all his fears. He looked to Jesus, and was filled with joy and peace in believing! By disobeying the commands of the law, you sin against divine majesty, but by disobeying the commands of the gospel, you sin against divine mercy. If indeed you remember your sins, and be deeply humbled, God has promised to forget them, and be reconciled to you.

God Invites You to accept of Pardon

The year of redemption is come. The trumpet of jubilee, in sweet and melodious tones, proclaims liberty to the captive, and the opening of the prison to them that are

REPENTANCE EXPLAINED AND ENFORCED

bound. Blessed are the people who know the joyful sound. Blessed is the man whose transgression is forgiven, and whose sin is covered. If the authority of God does not awe, let the kindness of God allure you. Do you think these tidings are too good to be true? While you linger, he sends forth messenger after messenger, with winning invitations and persuasions, to compel you to come in. It is the policy of hell to keep back the hungry, fainting soul from the rich provision of the gospel. Come, needy sinners, for all things are now ready.

> *Seek ye the LORD while he may be found, call upon him while he is near: Let the wicked forsake his way, and the unrighteous man his thoughts: and let him return unto the LORD, and he will have mercy upon him; and to our God, for he will abundantly pardon. (Isaiah 55:6 and 7).*

Do you cry out, wonderful condescension! Who could have thought of such goodness? Who could have believed such a report, without the clearest and strongest proofs? I reply, it is true this is not the manner of men.

> *For my thoughts are not your thoughts, neither are your ways my ways, saith the LORD. For as the heavens are higher than the earth, so are my ways higher than your ways, and my thoughts than your thoughts. (Isaiah 55:8 and 9).*

God not only invites you but,

(God) Pleads with You to accept Pardon

You do not need many arguments to persuade you to accept earthly blessings. And why is there not the same readiness to receive spiritual blessings? Hark! a voice softer than music, yet more majestic than the sound of many waters, addresses you.

> *Behold, I stand at the door, and knock: if any man hear my voice, and open the door, I will come in to*

CHAPTER 6: ENCOURAGEMENTS GIVEN TO THE PENITENT

him, and will sup with him, and he with me. (Revelation 3:20).

Perhaps you answer, Lord I am not worthy that thou shouldst come under my roof. I am all guilt and defilement. Wilt thou be a guest with one who deserves, if there were so many, a thousand hells? Hark! the same voice again speaks.

Come now, and let us reason together, saith the LORD: though your sins be as scarlet, they shall be as white as snow; though they be red like crimson, they shall be as wool. (Isaiah 1:18).

When the Lord of glory deigns to reason with you, and use such arguments, can you hold out in unbelief and remain unmoved? Were a king to go to a prison full of condemned criminals, and offer them pardon, do you think they would need many words to persuade them to accept it? I leave you both to answer the question, and make the application.

That you may be prevailed upon to receive pardon,

God Points You to the Blood of Atonement, by which it was procured

Jehovah could not dispense his mercy in any way that would dishonor his justice. The apostle therefore declares, that *without shedding of blood, there is no remission*. And how was satisfaction made? Was it with the blood of bulls, of goats, or of sheep? No! If the cattle upon a thousand hills had been all slain in sacrifice, they could not have made atonement for one sin. Look into the New Testament, and you will see Jesus freely giving himself up to die, that we might live. *For Christ also hath once suffered for sins, the just for the unjust, that he might bring us to God, being put to death in the flesh, but quickened by the Spirit. The chastisement of our peace was upon him; and with his stripes we are healed.* Think of the ransom that was paid; and then rejoice in the liberty procured by it.

> *In whom we have redemption through his blood, the forgiveness of sins, according to the riches of his grace. (Ephesians 1:7).*

In worldly matters, what is dearly bought, is, for the most part, diligently sought. Men dig in the mines for silver and gold, and dive in the sea for precious pearls; yet these things, however valued on account of their scarcity, have in them no real worth at all. But *ye were not redeemed with corruptible things, as silver and gold, But with the precious blood of Christ, as of a lamb without blemish and without spot*. O, who can calculate the price which bought thousands of millions of immortal souls! And do you not most ardently desire a pardon procured at so great an expense? Do you not thirst for a blessing which flows from such a spring of heavenly grace, through such a channel of heavenly redemption? If you are deaf to other calls, hear the voice of the Savior's blood. The blood of Abel cried for vengeance, and was heard; for God marked the murderer with his displeasure, and his punishment became intolerable. The blood of Christ cries for pardon and peace to penitents, and God seals them by the operation of his Holy Spirit.

That you may be prevailed upon to receive pardon,

God Points You to the Intercession of His Son

Were you sentenced to suffer a dreadful punishment for breaking the laws of your country, you would probably cry out, "O that I had a friend at court, to plead with his Majesty for me: I can expect no pardon, but from royal favor: yet I have no one to take up my cause, or speak on my behalf!" How would you be delighted to learn, that the king's own son was willing to become an intercessor for you!

CHAPTER 6: ENCOURAGEMENTS GIVEN TO THE PENITENT

For there is one God, and one mediator between God and men, the man Christ Jesus. The friend of helpless sinners says, *I am the way, the truth, and the life: no man cometh unto the Father, but by me.* These words claim the most serious attention. You may come to a fellow-creature, who invites, or you may send a denial; but you must come to God, or be eternally lost; for they that are far from him shall perish. There is but one way in which you can draw nigh to the Father, and that is through faith in his only-begotten Son. The apostle John says, *And if any man sin, we have an advocate with the Father, Jesus Christ the righteous.* And are you not willing to approach to God, in the new and living way of his own appointment? Dare you not trust your cause and your immortal soul in the hands of such an Advocate? He who prayed for his most cruel enemies while he hung on the cross, does not forget the poor and contrite, now that he sits upon the throne.

That you may be prevailed upon to receive pardon,

God Points You to Those Who have obtained the Precious Blessing

One would think the mere offer of forgiveness would be sufficient, without any arguments; but one extreme follows another, and the sinner is often hurried from presumption to the brink of despair. Is this your case? Do you cry, "Labor not to comfort me? I am lost and utterly undone. Surely, my condition is singular! none were ever so wicked as I am!" Be it so – did not Christ die to save the very chief of sinners? Were not Manasseh, Zacchaeus, Mary Magdalen, and the thief upon the cross, forgiven! The bloody Saul of Tarsus was arrested in his persecuting career, not to be dragged to torture and punishment, which were his due, but to be pardoned and sanctified. Nor was remission granted to him as an individual only, from whose experience others can derive no encouragement. Hear what he himself says:

REPENTANCE EXPLAINED AND ENFORCED

> *Howbeit for this cause I obtained mercy, that in me first Jesus Christ might shew forth all longsuffering, for a pattern to them which should hereafter believe on him to life everlasting. (1 Timothy 1:16).*

The apostle John declares, that *the blood of Jesus Christ his Son cleanseth us from all sin*. Surely, you dare not say this blood has lost its merit or its power! Could you look into heaven, you would see an immense multitude gathered out of all nations, many of whom were as vile as you are. There, they continually sing,

> *Unto him that loved us, and washed us from our sins in his own blood, And hath made us kings and priests unto God and his Father; to him be glory and dominion for ever and ever. Amen. (Revelation 1:5 and 6).*

If we have tasted the bitterness of repentance, the bitterness of the second death is past.

Let these reasons encourage you to draw nigh to God for pardon. Do you say, "I long for it. O that I knew my guilt were removed! O that my sins were freely forgiven me, for the Redeemer's sake!" I do not wonder at the anxiety you feel. Nothing can impart a relish of delight while the soul feels the anguish of conscious guilt, and finds no pardon. Archbishop Leighton justly observes, you cannot make a man joyful while he is oppressed with a heavy burden. Let gold and silver glisten before his eyes; let the sweetest music sooth his ears, and let dainties be prepared to feast his taste; still he groans and cries to be delivered from his burden. Thus it is with a soul oppressed with sin. Now, if you do long for pardon, what hinders you from enjoying the precious blessing? It is not that you are shut out by God, who is the Author of all spiritual comfort. I have read of a martyr who had his pardon placed by him in a box; and if he would deny his Lord, and renounce his profession, he was welcome to take it. But he nobly refused on such terms. When offered his choice to turn or burn, he

CHAPTER 6: ENCOURAGEMENTS GIVEN TO THE PENITENT

conferred not with flesh and blood, but followed truth, though at the expense of life itself. The case is here reversed. God has sent you a pardon, sealed by the blood of his Son. He has set it before you in the promises of the holy gospel. Poor trembling penitent! the devil would keep you from enjoying this invaluable blessing! And will you burn, in the fire this fiend kindles? O, fly to the Redeemer, and cast yourself before the throne of grace, and you shall hear him say, *Son or daughter, be of good cheer, thy sins are forgiven thee*! Such a word, as a token for good, is capable of scattering the most gloomy fears.

> *Comfort ye, comfort ye my people, saith your God. Speak ye comfortably to Jerusalem, and cry unto her, that her warfare is accomplished, that her iniquity is pardoned. (Isaiah 40:1 and 2).*

If there is any thing capable of making joy overflow all its banks, it is a strong persuasion of forgiveness coming after a deep sense of sin, and a full view of approaching punishment. I have read in history, of a certain nobleman, condemned to be beheaded for some crime, who, on receiving, just as he was led to execution, a pardon from the king, which he did not expect, was so transported that he died for joy! And when God grants a free and full pardon to you, ought not the liveliest pleasure to rise up within, and break out into strains of praise? He has manifested himself to you, that you may magnify him. Surely, your language ought to be,

> *Bless the LORD, O my soul, and forget not all his benefits: Who forgiveth all thine iniquities; who healeth all thy diseases; Who redeemeth thy life from destruction; who crowneth thee with lovingkindness and tender mercies. (Psalm 103:2-4).*

REPENTANCE EXPLAINED AND ENFORCED

THE SCRIPTURES OFFER TO THE PENITENT, ADOPTION INTO THE HOUSEHOLD OF GOD

It is a high favor for a king to grant pardon to a condemned traitor, so as to deliver him from death; but it is a far higher favor to admit him into his own palace, and raise him to enjoy a place of distinguished honor. But no instance of favor from one mortal to another, can equal the marvelous lovingkindness of God towards men. The greatest king on earth is but a few steps above the meanest beggar, or the most wretched outcast. Lord, what is man, that thou are mindful of him? The mercies of God are great, manifold, and unspeakable. Who can fathom the ocean, or measure the firmament? Who can count the dust of the earth, or the rays of the sun? Yet it were easier to fathom the depth of the ocean, or measure the extent of heaven; to count the dust of the earth, or the rays that stream from the sun, than to comprehend the infinite goodness, or sum up the numberless mercies of God. We are such poor, feeble creatures, and our understandings so very narrow, that we are soon lost and overwhelmed in considering subjects like this. That we may be more affected, the mercy of God is in the scriptures represented under such forms as bear some resemblance to our relations one with another.

While I am endeavoring to animate the hope of the penitent, I should be chargeable with great neglect, if I did not pay particular attention to our Lord's beautiful parable of the prodigal son. It was spoken on purpose to encourage those publicans and broken-hearted sinners, who listened to the word of Jesus. Behold the thoughtless youth, demanding his portion, and hastening his journey into a far country. Throwing the reins upon his lusts, he squanders his substance in riotous living among profligates and harlots. Want speedily follows waste, and misery springs from folly, as the serpent bursts from the egg of the cockatrice. Brought to poverty and disgrace, he becomes a

CHAPTER 6: ENCOURAGEMENTS GIVEN TO THE PENITENT

slave to a citizen, and goes into the field to feed his swine. But at this low ebb of his fortune, in this winter of adversity, where are those friends that flowed in with the full tide, and fluttered round him in the sun-shine of prosperity? Where are the companions who laughed, and drank, and danced with him in his noon-day frolics, and midnight revels? Ah! they flattered and stripped, and then mocked and forsook him. And when he came to himself, he said,

> *How many hired servants of my father's have bread enough and to spare, and I perish with hunger! I will arise and to my father, and will say unto him, Father, I have sinned against heaven, and before thee, And am no more worthy to be called thy son: make me as one of thy hired servants. (Luke 15:17-19).*

He had been acting a madman's part. Now his reason returns, and his soul is filled with sorrow and shame. But remembering whence he has fallen, he wisely resolves upon a return. No sooner does the father espy him, at a great distance, than his bowels of compassion yearn with the softest and kindest emotions. He runs with impatient fondness to meet and embrace him, and give him a hearty welcome. Servants are commanded to bring forth a ring, and the best robe, to kill the fatted calf, and prepare a feast of joy; for, saith the father,

> *This my son was dead, and is alive again; he was lost, and is found. (Luke 15:24).*

Take reader, this interesting parable, and consider it. It is a picture intended to represent, on the one hand, the sinner's folly; and on the other, our heavenly Father's mercy. And are you too, like the prodigal, come to your right mind? Is the frenzy that turned your brain abated? Do you see your soul stripped and undone? Do you look back, and sigh, and weep, at the remembrance of your ways and doings? Arise then and go to your Father, who is in heaven. His tender mercies continue to this moment. His house is open, and yet there is room. The lying enemy may tell you it is too late. Even your own heart may yield to fears and misgivings. But whither can you go? It is death to turn back to the world. While therefore God sits upon a throne of grace, go to him and plead your cause in the name of Jesus. I can assure you of a hearty welcome. Your rags shall be exchanged for the robe of righteousness and the garments of salvation. Instead of pining in want and misery, you shall sit down at a feast of gladness.

Adoption is a privilege of the greatest value. It confers the highest honor. Many think it a great thing to be related to an earthly prince. David was ready to shrink when the offer was made him to marry the daughter of Saul. He exclaimed, "Who am I, or what is my father's house, that I should be son-in-law to the king?" How much more may a Christian cry out, with wonder and gratitude, what am I, whose origin is in the dust, whose nature is corrupted, that I should call God my Father, and Christ my Savior? Yet all believers are sons and daughters of the Lord Almighty. The most exalted and envied titles of worldly men, are little better than empty sounds. To have a name and a place in God's house, is to rise far higher than the loftiest pinnacle of earthly greatness. Yet such honor have all the saints. While the apostle John considered this privilege, his mind was filled with admiration, and *fired* with holy rapture. He burst out in the language of devout gratitude,

> *Behold, what manner of love the Father hath bestowed upon us, that we should be called the sons of God: therefore the world knoweth us not, because it knew him not. (1 John 3:1).*

Besides honor, this privilege necessarily includes all that provision that we need. Surely, that God who supplies the beasts of the field with food, and feeds the fowls of the air, will not forget his own children. Their provision is secured to them in a covenant ordered in all things by infinite wisdom, and ratified by unchangeable promises.

CHAPTER 6: ENCOURAGEMENTS GIVEN TO THE PENITENT

God chooses their inheritance, fixes their lot, furnishes their table, guides and guards their walk. He gives grace and glory, and no good thing will he withhold from them that walk uprightly. The pampered and lordly worldling, who has his portion in this life is at his best estate altogether vanity. The believer may seem poor, and in the eyes of the thoughtless multitude he is often despised, but he is in reality, and in the estimate of heaven, peculiarly honorable.

> *For all things are yours; Whether Paul, or Apollos, or Cephas, or the world, or life, or death, or things present, or things to come; all are yours; And ye are Christ's; and Christ is God's. (1 Corinthians 3:21-23).*

When the Spanish ambassador went to see the famous treasury of St. Mark's, in Venice, he began to search and ask, if it had any bottom; because, said he, my master's treasures (by which he meant the mines of Peru) have no bottom. Vain boast! What was this, but the thorn vaunting over the thistle? Those once rich mines, it is well known, are now almost exhausted, and scarcely pay for the working. The Christian, indeed, has an enduring substance, an unfailing storehouse, a bottomless mine.

In virtue of their adoption, believers receive correction. Even a heathen could say, no man is more unhappy, than he to whom no affliction ever happened. *For whom the Lord loveth he chasteneth, and scourgeth every son whom he receiveth. (Hebrews 12:6).* And is it not a great advantage to be weaned from the world, and separated from folly? Is it not better to be corrected in measure, that we may be partakers of God's holiness, than to escape the rod, and be cut off by the sword of justice in our wickedness?

I shall add, that all who are adopted look forward to a glorious and eternal inheritance. If sons, then heirs, heirs of God, and joint-heirs with Christ. Oh, what a portion has

REPENTANCE EXPLAINED AND ENFORCED

the Lord laid up for his people! Death, which makes the worldling poor, gives the Christian admission into the best possessions. One of the Greek philosophers, being met by a person who asked him what he had lost in the fire that had burnt down the town and the house in which he lived, answered, "I have lost nothing, for I carry all my riches in myself."

A Christian can go much farther than he went, and say all my treasure is in heaven, under the keeping of the Almighty. I would not carry it with me if I might, for I know that it is in better hands. The believer, as one observes, should a fire consume the world, could stand upon its ashes, and say, "I have lost nothing." All who are now justified sinners in Christ, shall soon be glorified saints with Christ. Happy are they who can join with the apostle Peter,

> *Blessed be the God and Father of our Lord Jesus Christ, which according to his abundant mercy hath begotten us again unto a lively hope by the resurrection of Jesus Christ from the dead, To an inheritance incorruptible, and undefiled, and that fadeth not away, reserved in heaven for you.* (1 Peter 1:3 and 4).

Is adoption a privilege so valuable? Then let it be your great concern to possess it. How eager are many to gain acquaintance with great men. They struggle through the greatest difficulties to obtain a place of power, or a high sounding name. Can you say; Let the proud and ambitious seek the honor that comes from man? I wish above all things that honor which comes from God? May I have a place with his people, and I envy not those who hold the high places of the earth? To know that my name is in the book of life, will give me greater joy, than to be universally praised by men? If adoption secures such provision, do you not desire to belong to the household of faith? Whither can a child go in all its difficulties and distresses, but to a father? Now if you are adopted and received of God, you may approach him with a strong faith, and filial freedom. Are you in poverty? Go to God and entreat him to grant you from his fullness, those things that may be good for you. Are you in perplexity? Go to God for direction, and he shall guide you by his counsel. Are you in trouble? Go to God for relief and comfort, for as your day is so shall your strength be. If adoption stands connected with such glorious hopes, is it not a privilege worthy to be desired and sought? Yet a little while, and the Lord of glory will return to receive his people. Those who love him shall be as the sun, when he goeth forth in his might. The sun may for a time be clouded, but still shines more and more until the perfect day. Thus the saint may be for a while covered with reproach, and hid by the thick veil of poverty, but at last he shall shine with unspotted lustre as the sun without a cloud. When the Redeemer appears, all the sons of God will be made manifest, and shall be forever with and like their Lord.

THE SCRIPTURES PROMISE TO THE PENITENT THE INFLUENCE OF THE HOLY SPIRIT

It is a great favor to have sin pardoned and be saved from the wrath to come. It is a still greater favor to be adopted into the household of God, and made joint-heirs with Christ. But the greatest favor, and that which crowns and completes all the rest, is the gift of the Divine Spirit, to fit us for the sufferings and services below, and for happiness above. There must be holy dispositions to engage in holy duties, and heavenly desires to qualify us for heavenly delights. It is a good observation of a living writer, "when God calls an angel, to employ him, he is fit for the work; but when God calls a sinful mortal into his presence, he has to prepare him for his service." And how is this fitness for obeying and enjoying God to be obtained, but by his own gracious influence?

REPENTANCE EXPLAINED AND ENFORCED

> *Now he that hath wrought us for the selfsame thing is God, who also hath given unto us the earnest of the Spirit. (2 Corinthians 5:5).*

When Solomon dedicated the temple, he burst out into these words. *But will God indeed dwell on the earth? behold, the heaven and heaven of heavens cannot contain thee; how much less this house that I have builded? (1 Kings 8:27).* Now you may be ready to say, the temple of Solomon was a glorious place, but who am I? Will God indeed so much as look upon such a worthless worm? Will the Majesty of heaven dwell with me, the chief of sinners? Your fellow-creatures, I grant, when they are raised a little above you, are apt to turn away their eyes from you with scorn and contempt. But God remembers you, in your low estate, for his mercy endureth forever.

> *Thus saith the LORD, The heaven is my throne, and the earth is my footstool: For all those things hath mine hand made, but to this man will I look, even to him that is poor and of a contrite spirit, and trembleth at my word. (Isaiah 66:1 and 2).*

Sweet encouragement! With one look of love and compassion from God, you need not fear, though all the envious and malicious eyes in the world were fixed upon you, and all the forces of earth and hell stand against you. Amidst fightings without, and fears within, you may be sometimes depressed and disconsolate. When therefore you are ready to faint, seek a cordial in these animating words.

> *For thus saith the high and lofty One that inhabiteth eternity, whose name is Holy; I dwell in the high and holy place, with him also that is of a contrite and humble spirit, to revive the spirit of the humble, and to revive the heart of the contrite ones. (Isaiah 57:15).*

Nor is the language of the New Testament on this point less encouraging than that of the Old. It seems

CHAPTER 6: ENCOURAGEMENTS GIVEN TO THE PENITENT

strange to me, that any one can read the Holy Scriptures with the least degree of serious attention, and deny the all-important doctrine of the Divine Spirit's influence. There is scarcely a truth in the Bible more plainly and abundantly taught. Our Lord on this subject makes a powerful and moving appeal to the most tender feelings of human nature.

> Or what man is there of you, whom if his son ask bread, will he give him a stone? Or if he ask a fish, will he give him a serpent? (Matthew 7:9 and 10).

No; impossible. He who could mock the wants of his own child, rather than supply them, is worse than a beast, harder than a flint, a monster more hateful than the old serpent himself.

> If ye then, being evil, know how to give good gifts unto your children: how much more shall your heavenly Father give the Holy Spirit to them that ask him? (Luke 11:13).

If it be asked for what purpose this precious gift is bestowed, I answer, it is the office of the Holy Spirit to enlighten, to sanctify and comfort the soul.

It is the Office of the Holy Spirit to Enlighten the Soul

It has been justly said, the sun shines as much on the poor man's cottage, as on the prince's palace. The scriptures declare, that not many of the wise, the mighty, and the noble are called, but God hath chosen the foolish things of the world to confound the wise; and God hath chosen the weak things of the world to confound the things that are mighty. 1 Corinthians 1:27 and 28. I shall venture, therefore, to carry the figure just mentioned a little further. The natural sun shines more upon the high mountains than upon the deep inclosed vales; but the Sun of Righteousness sheds his cheering beams on those who walk in the valley of humiliation, and withholds them from the high and lofty. All true wisdom comes from above. Ministers may describe

REPENTANCE EXPLAINED AND ENFORCED

its excellency and use, but God alone can impart it. As easily might man give the faculty of understanding to an idiot, as give spiritual discernment to one who is hoodwinked with the bandages of carnal blindness.

> But if our gospel be hid, it is hid to them that are lost: In whom the god of this world hath blinded the minds of them which believe not, lest the light of the glorious gospel of Christ, who is the image of God, should shine unto them. (2 Corinthians 4:3 and 4).

Now the Holy Spirit was promised for this very purpose, to take of the things of Christ, and show them unto us. And do you desire to obtain divine knowledge? Do you long to be made wise unto salvation through faith which is in Jesus Christ? Be not content with the teaching of men, but look up to God, that he may turn darkness into light before you. With faith and fervency, patience and perseverance, pray that he may give you his Holy Spirit to guard you from every error in doctrine and practice, and guide you into all truth.

It is the Office of the Holy Spirit to Sanctify the Soul

His sacred influence is compared to water and fire, which cleanse and purify. Without holiness, it is expressly said, no man shall see the Lord. Outward means alone cannot produce purity of heart. If, then, you think you can either enter the bright mansions of glory without holiness, or become truly holy without the washing of regeneration and the renewing of the Holy Ghost, you will find yourself awfully mistaken. Christians are said to be partakers of the divine nature. When we behold the proud becoming humble, and the profane pious, we have living proofs of the Spirit's influence. Hence, when Paul writes to the Corinthians, and mentions idolaters, adulterers, thieves, drunkards, revilers, and extortioners, he says,

> And such were some of you: but ye are washed, but ye are sanctified, but ye are justified in the name of

CHAPTER 6: ENCOURAGEMENTS GIVEN TO THE PENITENT

> *the Lord Jesus, and by the Spirit of our God. (1 Corinthians 6:11).*

And can similar effects be produced in our day, by any other than the same cause? Is the Spirit of the Lord straitened? Is the hand of the Lord shortened, that it cannot save, or is the ear of the Lord heavy, that it cannot hear? Is the promise of God, as a covenant out of date, or is the fountain of grace now empty? If there were not good grounds to hope for the same sanctifying influences, which the first Christians experienced, your case would be desperate. The words spoken by the Lord to the prophet, concerning Ephraim, would be applicable.

> *Ephraim is joined to idols: let him alone. (Hosea 4:17).*

O, dreadful state! To be given up to a reprobate mind, to work all uncleanness with greediness, is the most wretched condition this side of hell! Does your blood chill, and your soul tremble at the thought? Then I am persuaded better things of you, and things which accompany salvation, though I thus speak. Look and pray to God for his sanctifying grace. He who so plentifully poured forth the divine influences on the day of Pentecost, has the residue of the Spirit to impart. And will you not then seek it? The hope of forgiveness to one who dreads future punishment, and the gracious means of sanctification to one who hates sin, ought to make the heart bound with joy. O, put the language of penitent David into prayer for yourself.

> *Create in me a clean heart, O God; and renew a right spirit within me. Cast me not away from thy presence; and take not thy holy spirit from me. (Psalm 51:10 and 11).*

It is the Office of the Holy Spirit to Comfort the Soul

Some there are who look at religion only on the unfavorable side. They see the fire and hear the tempest,

REPENTANCE EXPLAINED AND ENFORCED

but hear not the still, small voice. Now, though religion may cause grief, it is such as must issue in gladness. As Jesus Christ is termed the Consolation of Israel, so the Divine Spirit is called the Comforter. He does indeed wound and pierce the heart, but his title is from that part of his work which yields the believer peace and joy. Christ represents his sacred influence, as even more necessary to the disciples than his own personal presence.

> *Nevertheless I tell you the truth; It is expedient for you that I go away: for if I go not away, the Comforter will not come unto you; but if I depart, I will send him unto you. (John 16:7).*

The Holy Spirit is promised to strengthen your faith, scatter your fears, and revive your hopes. By his assistance, you shall taste that the Lord is gracious, and quitting every vain refuge, firmly lay hold on eternal life. With his help, you shall experience both the pleasure and profit of religion. Well did Jesus say,

> *Blessed are the poor in spirit: for theirs is the kingdom of heaven. Blessed are they that mourn: for they shall be comforted. (Matthew 5:3 and 4).*

Wheresoever the Holy Spirit dwells, these words are fulfilled. If you doubt this, appeal to the experience of devout Christians. To which of the saints will you go? They will, as with one voice, assure you, that rich consolation flows from the living spring of divine influence in the mind. O, seek the Holy Spirit to visit and cheer you. Pray that he may abide with you forever. Is there a burden which this Comforter cannot lighten? a bitter cup which he cannot heal? a want which he cannot supply? a woe which he cannot remove? O, how thankful ought we to be for the promise of the Spirit. Should you hear, for the sake of religion, the defaming of many, the hiss of scorn, and the clamor of prejudice and pride around you, the Comforter would be there with you. No walls or bars can exclude him. The holy John Bradford, who suffered martyrdom in the

CHAPTER 6: ENCOURAGEMENTS GIVEN TO THE PENITENT

reign of the bigoted and bloody queen Mary, wrote to inform his friends that he had enjoyed the happiest days in his prison that ever he had enjoyed in his whole life. Be earnest in seeking the comfortable testimony of the Spirit, witnessing with your spirit, the privilege of adoption; and then neither the world nor the devil can rob you of your confidence. O, the sweet peace! the cheering hope! the transporting joy! which flow from the grace of the Lord Jesus Christ, the love of God, and the communion of the Holy Spirit.

SET THESE ENCOURAGEMENTS BEFORE YOU

To Quicken You in Your Duties, and Animate You Amidst all Your Fears and Foes

They may serve to quicken you in duties. It is not a light matter to enter upon the service of God. He appoints the work you have to do, and the time in which it must be done. He lays down his commands as your rule, and makes the promotion of his own glory your end. You must wait upon him, and look to him. He needs not your obedience, but yet he requires, and in a certain sense, rewards it.

> But they that wait upon the LORD shall renew their strength; they shall mount up with wings as eagles; they shall run, and not be weary; and they shall walk, and not faint. (Isaiah 40:31).

The melting penitent must become an obedient servant. It is better to belong to what a venerable bishop calls the holy order of mourners in Zion, than to move in the first ranks of those giddy mirth-making worldlings, who get all their good things in this life, and afterwards are tormented. If you grieve for your own sins, and sigh and cry for the abominations around you, God will set a mark upon you, that you may be spared when the scourge of destruction comes.

They that sow in tears shall reap in joy. But there is a considerable space between the seed-time and the

REPENTANCE EXPLAINED AND ENFORCED

harvest. You may wait many wintry days and cold chilling nights, but the promise cannot fail. And O, what joy will follow the transient sorrows of time.

> *For yet a little while, and he that shall come will come, and will not tarry. (Hebrews 10:37).*

Think within yourself, are not all the promises of God yea and Amen in Christ Jesus? Men have often deceived me, but the God of faithfulness will not forget his Word. My heart has often deceived me, but God is greater than my heart, and knoweth all things. As he hath promised pardon, I will ask him to bestow it. The blessing has been sealed in the well-ordered and unchangeable covenant; O, that it were applied to my conscience, and sealed by his gracious hand upon my melting heart! As he hath set before me an open door into the household of faith, I will go in and sit down with Abraham, and Isaac, and Jacob, in the kingdom of heaven. As the residue of the Spirit is with him, I will seek an abundant and an abiding measure of his heavenly influence. This is the best method I can recommend to you, for the attainment of true comfort. Be not afraid you will offend God by your earnestness. You are not only exhorted to come boldly to a throne of grace, but also to wrestle, till, like Jacob, you prevail and win the blessing.

These encouragements may serve,

To Support You Amidst all Your Foes and Fears

Sometimes you may be ready to draw back from the prospect of trials. You may begin to say within yourself, shall I not now be forsaken and despised? Are there not mountains of difficulties to climb, and seas of trouble to pass? What will my old companions think? What will the world say, that I now give up my time to religion? Never mind what the world thinks or says on this subject. I can tell you what pious men will say: Behold a brand plucked out of the fire! What hath God wrought! This is the Lord's doing, and it is marvelous in our eyes! Come, poor

CHAPTER 6: ENCOURAGEMENTS GIVEN TO THE PENITENT

penitent, come with us, and we will do thee good, for God hath spoken good concerning Israel. I can tell you what every faithful minister will say: "Now I rejoice, not that you are made sorrowful, but that you sorrow after a godly sort." There are many kinds of grief which are deadly, but this sort is the spring of life. I can almost venture to tell you what the angels say. Methinks I hear them crying to each other, Strike your golden harps, for another heir of heaven is born. Glory to God in the highest, and on earth, peace and good will to men! Is this mere fancy? No; He who knows all things, hath said, There is joy in the presence of the angels of God, over one sinner that repenteth. Those bright beings take especial pleasure in every thing which advances the welfare of man. We never read of their rejoicing at the downfall of cities long besieged, or victories bought with torrents of blood; it is the conversion of a sinner which creates a triumph in heaven. I can tell you what Jesus Christ says, Come unto me, weary, heavy laden sinner, and I will give thee rest. Thou hast found it hard to kick against the pricks, but my yoke is easy. In the world thou shalt have tribulation, but in me, peace.

With these encouragements,

Set Your Hand to the Covenant of God, and Solemnly Surrender your Soul to Him

Is it not a great matter that Jehovah is ready to receive you? Peace is made by the blood of the cross; you have nothing to do but accept the blessing, and adore the giver of it. God says, "Seek ye my face," and does not your heart reply, "Thy face, Lord, will I seek!" There is a covenant which secures ten thousand precious blessings to you, and gives the whole undivided praise to God. He who has bought you, and called you, claims you as his own, and requires you to serve him with your body and your spirit, which are his.

REPENTANCE EXPLAINED AND ENFORCED

And I will betroth thee unto me for ever; yea, I will betroth thee unto me in righteousness, and in judgment, and in lovingkindness, and in mercies. I will even betroth thee unto me in faithfulness: and thou shalt know the LORD. (Hosea 2:19 and 20).

Does God confirm the sacred covenant with so many seals? Does he bind you to himself with so many ties? And ought you not to feel and acknowledge your obligations? O, come and yield up your soul to him. In the most solemn and deliberate manner, make a full and absolute surrender of all you have, and all you are, into his hands. Let your language be, "O God, I had sold myself to sin, and was enslaved by Satan, and the present evil world. Thou hast redeemed me, and at thy footstool I bow myself with entire submission. Other lords, besides thee, have had dominion over me, but now by thee only will I make mention of thy name. Thou are my God, and I will praise thee; my father's God, and I will exalt thee. "Whatsoever thou choosest me to be, to have, to want, to do, or to suffer, I cheerfully acquiesce in thy wise and righteous appointments." Instruct me to know thy will, and assist me to do it. O, my Father, I now join myself to thee in a perpetual covenant, never to be forgotten! I had rather be a door-keeper in thy house, than dwell in the tents of wickedness. Let me but feel thy supporting hand, hear thy gracious voice, and see thy reconciled countenance, and I can go on my way rejoicing. O, thou Prince of life! thou Lover and Savior of men! receive a worthless sinner. Thou only art my master, my guide, my deliverer, my portion! May I never, no never, deny or dishonor thee. O, Holy Spirit of grace! I desire to resign myself to thy quickening, illuminating, and sanctifying power. Take possession of my soul. Turn out every rival, and reign over all my affections with uncontrolled authority. Prepare me for every good word and work on earth, and for everlasting joy in heaven.

Such a solemn covenant-engagement as this may leave a lasting and favorable impression on the mind. In

CHAPTER 6: ENCOURAGEMENTS GIVEN TO THE PENITENT

future days, it may be profitable to review it, and repeat your vows. Nor let it be thought, there is any thing singular in making such a covenant with God. David thus bound his treacherous heart:

> "O my soul, thou has said unto the Lord, Thou art **my Lord**." Paul thus surrendered himself to the Redeemer, and could say, "I know whom I have believed, and am persuaded that he is able to keep that which I have committed unto him against that day."

When the disciples of Socrates brought rich presents to him, as proofs of their regard and affection, there was one who said, "I am poor, and having no property, I give you all I have, I give up myself to you." Socrates answered, "Thou couldest not have brought me a more acceptable present. I receive the gift, and I will restore thee back to thyself, better than when I received thee." You cannot carry any offering to Christ so pleasing to him as yourself. He is your sole Master. Socrates was but a glimmering taper, amidst surrounding darkness; Christ is the great Sun of Righteousness. He will teach you freely, and save you fully. You must, however, give yourself to him, not for a few years only, but forever. If you continue in his word, and keep his covenant now, you shall hereafter dwell in his immediate presence, in the mansions of unsullied glory.

PRAYERS

PRAYER FOR EXAMINATION

Eternal God, the great Searcher of hearts, who knowest all our secret thoughts, and from whose all-seeing eye nothing is hid, dispose me frequently to examine the state of my mind, and to compare mine actions with the rule of thy laws, that nothing contrary to thy holy will may ever find a settled abode in my soul; and let me so consider my ways, as to turn my feet unto thy testimonies, to repent, and to live. Grant that I may so impartially judge and condemn myself, that I may not be condemned at thy dreadful tribunal. Let not self-love impose upon me in a matter of such high importance; let not sloth and negligence deter me from keeping mine accounts clear and spotless; let no darling passion be so far indulged, as to escape the scrutiny of serious examination: and whenever, O Lord, I have discovered mine own vileness, grant that, by the assistance of thy grace, I may humble myself under a proper sense of it before thee; that I may from my heart condemn all those follies, by which I have so justly provoked thy wrath and indignation against me; that I may earnestly solicit thy pardon and forgiveness through the merits of my Redeemer; that I may be careful to stand upon my guard for the future; and by prayer and watchfulness engage thy powerful protection, which is so necessary to support me in the time of temptation, the day of trial, and the awful hour of death. Grant this, O Lord, for the sake of Jesus Christ, mine only Mediator and Advocate. Amen.

FOR TRUE CONTRITION

Most gracious God, full of compassion, long-suffering, and of great pity, who sparest when we deserve punishment, and in thy wrath thinkest upon mercy; cause me earnestly to repent, and heartily to be sorry for all my misdoings: make the remembrance of them so burdensome and painful to me, that I may flee to thee with a trouble spirit, and a contrite heart. Forgive me all the sins which I can now call to remembrance; and forgive me likewise all my transgressions of thy holy will, which may now be out of the reach of my memory, but which have been open to thine all-seeing eye, and are known to thee with all their circumstances and aggravations. Pardon me, O Lord, according to the abundant goodness of thy nature, and the declarations made by thy Son Jesus Christ; and grant me that forgiveness which I can neither ask nor expect, but upon those terms and conditions which thy holiness and mercy have laid down in the gospel. And as I am truly sensible that no forgiveness can be expected, according to thy Word, without amendment of life, I seriously renounce all communication with whatever is displeasing to thee, and sincerely resolve to make it my great endeavor to correct every thing that is amiss in my temper and behavior, and to bring myself still nearer to thy holiness and perfection. Forgive me, therefore, as thou hast promised by thy dearly-beloved Son; visit, comfort, and relieve me; cast me not away from thy presence, and take not thy *Holy Spirit from me; but excite in me true repentance and contrition; give me knowledge of thy truth, and confidence in thy mercy; and in the world to come, life everlasting, for the sake of Jesus Christ, my Lord and Savior. *Amen.*

* The Holy Spirit in the New Testament Church age seals the born-again believer and is never taken away as in the Old Testament dispensations. See Ephesians 1:13 and 14, 4:30; 2 Corinthians 1:22, etc.

FOR PARDON

Most gracious God, who desireth not the death of a sinner, but rather that he should turn from his wickedness and live; unto thee I present my humble supplications, not only for mercy to pardon my past offences, but also for

REPENTANCE EXPLAINED AND ENFORCED

grace to assist me in times of future need. Create in me a clean heart, and renew a right spirit within me. Make me to reflect on my ways, to turn my feet unto thy testimonies, and wherein I have done amiss to do so no more. Give me that godly sorrow which worketh repentance unto salvation not to be repented of. Lead me not into temptation, but deliver me from evil; and grant that I may finally come off conqueror, yea more than conqueror, through him who hath loved us. Forgetting those things that are behind, may I press forward to the mark for the prize of the high calling of God in Christ Jesus? Let not my goodness be as the morning cloud, or the early dew, which passeth away; but may it be as the shining light, which shineth more and more unto the perfect day. Finally, let no iniquity have dominion over me; but may I be steadfast, immovable, always abounding in the work of the Lord, forasmuch as I know that my labor will not then be in vain. Grant this, O God, for the sake of Jesus Christ.   *Amen.*

FOR GRACE

Gracious God, who hast promised to give thy Holy Spirit to them that ask; vouchsafe unto me, I beseech thee, its all powerful influence to cleanse my polluted nature, to comfort me in all my troubles, to succor me in temptations, and to assist me in the discharge of my duty, that I may be enabled to walk in thy faith and fear all the days of my life. To thy gracious protection I commit my soul, O thou that art faithful, as well as good; watch over me, therefore, that I be not beguiled by the deceitfulness of sin, by the contagion of mine own corrupt heart, or the malice of my spiritual enemies; but may I so watch and pray that I enter not into temptation; and after having lived the life of grace here, may inherit thy glory hereafter, in another and a better world, for the sake of Jesus Christ.   *Amen.*

FOR PREPARATION FOR ETERNITY

Lord God Almighty, who hast ordained this life as a passage to the future, by confining our conversion to the time of our pilgrimage here, and reserving for hereafter the state of punishment and reward; vouchsafe me the assistance of thy grace, who still have an opportunity of reconcilement to thee, that I may so watch over all mine actions, and correct every deviation in my way to heaven, as neither to be surprised with my sins uncancelled, nor called away with my duties unperformed; but that, when my body descendeth to the grave, my soul may ascend to thee, and dwell for ever in those mansions of eternal felicity, which are prepared for all thy faithful servants, through the merits of Jesus Christ, thy Son, our Lord. *Amen.*

APPENDIX

BACKGROUND

This New Haven 1834 original edition of *Repentance: Enforced and Explained* was obtained by Solid Rock Baptist Church of Calgary through a personal search into specified archives. The Title Page of the book was signed by a Mr. Edwin F. Hatfield of New York in 1848. The book was subsequently given as a gift by the children of Edwin Hatfield to the Library of Union Theological Seminary, New York, at an unspecified date.

The importance of this book was immediately recognized. The goal of republishing this classic work was to preserve the original edition, in a modern copy format. The publication of this treatise involved re-typing the entire manuscript by Frank Crawford without any change in the original wording, except where occasional printing errors in the general text and scriptural references occurred. They are attributed to the printing process rather than the author, J. Thornton.

A more-detailed Table of Contents for *Repentance: Enforced and Explained* allows the reader easy access to Mr. Thornton's thorough examination of the doctrine of Repentance. The sections and sub-sections are highlighted in the book's text. All scripture quotations are from the AV 1611 Bible.

RELATED STUDY ITEMS ON THE OLD PATHS PUBLICATIONS WEBSITE

The interested reader is referred to *The Technique Catastrophe* by Bob Creel. The theme of this excellent book underlines the vital importance of Biblical repentance in witnessing as opposed to the man-made methods being used in many churches today.

APPENDIX

The following tracts in the Articles section of our website may be of interest also:

A Call to National Repentance

The Technique Catastrophe (Condensed from the above book)

Repentance: Enforced and Explained (Condensed from the book)

(These tracts can be found on this webpage: http://theoldpathspublications.com/Pages/Articles.htm)

www.ingramcontent.com/pod-product-compliance
Lightning Source LLC
Chambersburg PA
CBHW032125090426
42743CB00007B/476